The World of Human Rights

About the Author

Jhumpa Mukherjee, M.A. (Gold Medalist), PhD is an Assistant Professor of Political Science at St. Xavier's College, Kolkata. She is a member of the Centre for Decentralization and Rural Development, Rabindra Bharati University, Kolkata. She has published articles on Contemporary social and political issues in nationally acclaimed journals and has participated in national seminars. Her areas of research interest include South Asian Politics, Human Rights, and multicultural governance in federal systems.

The World of Human Rights

Jhumpa Mukherjee

CONCEPT PUBLISHING COMPANY PVT. LTD.
NEW DELHI-110059

ISBN-13 : 978-93-5125-098-2

First Published 2014

Published and Printed by

Concept Since 1974

Concept Publishing Company Pvt. Ltd.
A/15-16, Commercial Block, Mohan Garden
New Delhi-110059 (India)
T: 25351460, 25351794, *F*: 091-11-25357109
E: publishing@conceptpub.com, W: www.conceptpub.com
Editorial Office: H-13, Bali Nagar, New Delhi-110 015, India.

Cataloging in Publication Data—*Courtesy:* D.K. Agencies (P) Ltd. <docinfo@dkagencies.com>

Mukherjee, Jhumpa.
The world of human rights / Jhumpa Mukherjee.
p. cm.
Includes bibliographical references (p.) and index.
ISBN 9789351250982

1. Human rights. I. Title.

DDC 323 23

Preface

The post-cold war international system is marked by a renewed interest in human rights. With new humanitarian crises and newer patterns of human rights violations, national and international agencies have felt the need for a better understanding and protection of human rights. Since the last two decades especially, if not more, governments and non-governmental agencies have been attempting to create a human rights' culture for society, to define basic dignity and worth of human beings. Policy makers and academicians feel that denial of basic human rights and freedoms not only cause individual discomfort but also create conditions of social and political unrest.

The recent spurt in social movements are an attempt to reinforce consciousness and awareness of potential violations in different fields, so much so that these movements on issues of environment, gender, tribal rights, peace, *dalits* have one thing in common—violation of rights of these segments. With growing awareness, the concept of human rights has taken the shape of a full-fledged discipline today. Human Rights have emerged as an independent, autonomous discipline taught at undergraduate and postgraduate levels in most institutions in India and abroad.

The National Commission on Human Rights set up under the Protection of Human Rights Act, 1993 has come out with a detailed syllabus on the need of inculcating and educating the young generation to create a violation free world.

The present book is an attempt to systematically combine the different concepts and mechanisms and issues of human rights in a lucid manner to cater to the needs of graduate and post-graduate students.

I take this opportunity to express my sincere gratitude to my friends, family and colleagues for their continuous support and cooperation. A special thanks to my students of Human Rights classes who would never be tired of asking questions and in the process help me rethink the issues from a different perspective. I am extremely grateful to Maa and Baba who had always taught me to give my best in whatever I do.

My sincere appreciation to Mr. Ashok Kumar Mittal of Concept Publishing Company Pvt. Ltd. and the editorial team for their guidance and support in the entire process of publication.

Jhumpa Mukherjee

Contents

Contents

Section I

[illegible] Human Rights

Section II

[illegible] Human Rights

Section I
The Fundamentals of Human Rights

1

Understanding Human Rights and Duties

1.1 Defining Human Rights

Human rights belong to everyone of us without exception. But unless we know them, unless we demand they be respected, and unless we defend our right — and the right of others — to exercise them, they will be just words in a decades-old document. This simple message by the Secretary-General of United Nations, Ban Ki-Moon on the occasion of World Human Rights Day, 2011 was addressed to the people of all countries, because human rights are to be enjoyed by one and all regardless of any consideration. Awareness of human rights is essential as a tool for the observance and promotion of human rights and for creation of an environment of public opinion in which gross violations of human rights are unacceptable. It is undeniable that while education and knowledge of human rights cannot totally prevent the violation of human rights, it can create moral and mental inhibitions and a sense of shame on the part of perpetrators of human rights and thus contribute to an improved environment of human rights.

What is it, then, that gives human rights a unique standing amongst political values and such international official recognition? The world of today is obsessed with human rights. It is the buzzword in both international and national domain. What is the basis for the consensus around human rights principles? Are these principles related to states? Why have human rights become a symbol for expressing individual and collective aspirations?

In this chapter, we answer some of these questions. We start with the basic question why are rights called 'human'?

The feeling of being a human being is a precondition to the enjoyment of rights. The very fact that one is a human being leads automatically to a belief that in order to live a decent life, he should enjoy certain choice, freedom and not be subjected to others commands, because every individual aspires to live a dignified life free from bondage and slavery. The idea of human rights is basically a political idea with a moral foundation. It implies certain individual entitlements and obligations with corresponding obligations on the part of the state. Implicit in the idea of human rights is the commitment to individual dignity and equality, as opposed to societal discrimination.

Human rights could, then, be defined as those rights which are inherent in our nature and without which we cannot live as human beings. Human rights and fundamental freedoms allow us to develop completely and utilize our human qualities, our intelligence and our conscience to satisfy our spiritual and other needs. It is a right of maintaining and enjoying human dignity and worth. It comprises of rights of individuals and groups circumscribing all spheres of life.

With the growing popularity of human rights agenda, a number of terminologies are associated with the concept—*fundamental rights, basic rights, natural rights, elementary rights*. There is no set pattern or uniform practice in the usages of these terms but all of these interrelated terms highlight the importance and worth of human freedom. These are fundamental because they are minimum entitlements that governments must promote and protect. "They are fundamental in the sense that they are given priority in social policy, administration and enactment of law, they are fundamental part of the law of the land and they are protected in many national systems by constitutional provisions and procedures, such as the equality of all before the law".[1] They are basic since they are essential for the very existence of man; they are natural as they were enjoyed by men even before the state came into existence.

Essentials of Human Rights

- It is a right of individuals to be exercised individually or collectively.
- These rights are inalienable.
- It is permanent and universal.
- These rights are minimum requirements for survival of mankind.
- They are protected and enforced by the State at all levels.

1.2 Tracing the Roots of Human Rights

There is no doubt that the term 'human rights' is a twentieth century buzzword. However, the idea of the inalienable rights of man is much older and was often articulated by philosophers and politicians since the distant past. The genesis of human rights may be traced from the days of Greeks in their notion of natural rights. The doctrine of natural rights rests on the belief that men enjoyed certain inalienable rights of life, liberty and property, even before the coming of the State.

In the medieval period, that is, from the thirteenth century till the Treaty of Westphalia (1648), encompassing the period of Renaissance, certain basic changes took place in society creating the urge for basic human rights. It was during this period when events like religious intolerance and political-economic bondage began that people started clamouring for rights and freedom. The Magna Carta (1215), the Petition of Rights (1628) and the English Bill of Rights (1689) were proof of increasing awareness about the need for basic rights. However, the modern view of natural rights took a concrete shape only during the 17th and 18th century—the materialism of Hobbes, the rationalism of Rene Descartes and G.W.Leibniz, the pantheism of Spinoza—encouraged a belief in the inalienability of natural rights. Human rights got philosophical treatment in the writings of the English philosopher John Stuart

Mill (On Liberty) and of the American political theorist Thomas Paine (The Rights of Man). Awareness of rights was also reflected in the writings of Hobbes in his *Leviathan*, Locke in his *Two Treatises on Government* and Rousseau in his *Contract Sociale* through his notion of *vox populi vox dei*. The teachings of these liberal thinkers had a profound influence in the Western world during the eighteenth and nineteenth centuries which paved the way for the American War of Independence and the French Revolution. The American Declaration of Independence (1776) stated: "We hold these truths to be self-evident that all men are created equal, that they are endowed by (their) creator with certain inalienable rights; that among these are Life, Liberty and the Pursuit of Happiness". Along similar lines, the French Declaration of Rights of Man (1789) categorically stated that, "men are born free and remain equal in rights."

The notion of rights became popular but was still confined to the sweet will of the rulers. It was only after the First World War and the intense suffering that it brought along; that the realization dawned for the establishment of some institutional mechanism for the protection of the rights of man. The birth of the League of Nations was the first such modest attempt in this direction. However, the League directly did not provide for any provision for human rights but made indirect reference to the welfare of the people governed under the mandate. Article 22(1) reads, "the well-being and development of such people form a sacred trust of civilization". Until 1945, international response towards human rights was concentrated towards protecting particular groups in some countries, that is to say, it did not have a universal appeal. It was only after the United Nations Charter was signed in 1945 that an attempt was made to provide a comprehensive system for protection and promotion of human rights. The member states unanimously stressed the urgency of international efforts in encouraging respect for human rights and fundamental freedoms.

The dreadfulness of the Second World War was the prime motivating factor in pursuing the goals of protection of human rights in the post-war period. The United Nations, born out of the ruins of the Great War put utmost emphasis in fostering rights and freedoms. Specifically, the UN Charter was the first international instrument which, in unequivocal terms proclaimed "universal respect for, and observance of human rights and fundamental freedoms for all without distinction as to race, sex, language or religion". The Charter made promotion of human rights as one of its basic purposes and entrusted upon the member states to take joint and separate action in cooperation with the United Nations for the achievement of this purpose. Thus, the UN ushered in a new regime of human rights; until then human rights was the exclusive purview of states and individuals within its territory. For the first time in the history of mankind, human rights was internationalized and universalized.

International Bill of Human Rights

Although the UN Charter emphasized the need for promotion and protection of human rights, it did not endeavour to enumerate or define them. The task was left to the competent organs of the UN: the General Assembly, the Economic and Social Council, the Commission on Human Rights and their subsidiary bodies. In time, these bodies worked together to produce an impressive series of international human rights instruments, the most important of which is the International Bill of Human Rights consisting of Universal Declaration of Human Rights, International Covenant on Civil and Political Rights, the International Covenant on Social, Economic and Cultural Rights and the Optional Protocol to the International Covenant on Civil and Political Rights, the Second Optional Protocol to the International Covenant on Civil and Political Rights and the Optional Protocol to the International Covenant on Economic, Social and Cultural Rights.

1.3 The Universal Declaration of Human Rights (UDHR)

The Universal Declaration of Human Rights (UDHR) is one of the first international documents to be based on the idea that rights are guaranteed to each human being. Like the UN itself, the UDHR was written with the aim of establishing world peace by promoting human rights. Originally, the UDHR brought together 58 distinct geographic, cultural and political backgrounds in the formation of one universal document.[2] The Universal Declaration of Human Rights was drafted between January 1947 and December 1948. Its text was composed by the then eight-member Commission on Human Rights headed by Eleanor Roosevelt, and sought to include the whole spectrum of human rights: from cultural, social and economic to civil and political rights. Following over 1,400 votes modifying the document's text, the UN General Assembly unanimously passed the Declaration on December 10, 1948, with eight abstentions to the vote, coming from Belarus, Czechoslovakia, Poland, Saudi Arabia, South Africa, the Soviet Union, Ukraine, and Yugoslavia.

It was envisaged "as a common standard of achievement for all peoples and all nations. It is true that the Declaration did not have binding enforceability, yet it was a remarkable achievement. It is considered as customary international law and is widely accepted. It was the first occasion on which the organized community of nations had made a declaration of human rights and fundamental freedoms.

The UDHR consists of a Preamble and 30 Articles setting forth the basic human rights and fundamental freedoms to which all men and women everywhere in the world are entitled, without discrimination.

Article 1 and Article 2 lays down the philosophical underpinnings of human rights.

Article 1: All human beings are born free and equal in dignity and rights. They are endowed with reason and conscience and should act towards one another in a spirit of brotherhood.

Article 2: Everyone is entitled to all the rights and freedoms set forth in this Declaration, without distinction of any kind, such as, race, colour, sex, language, religion, political or other opinion, national or social origin, property, birth or other status.

Furthermore no distinction shall be made on the basis of the political, jurisdictional or international status of the country or territory to which a person belongs, whether it be independent trust, non-self-governing or under any other limitation of sovereignty.

Articles 3 to 21 provide for a list of civil and political rights necessary for the fullest development of human personality

Article 3: Everyone has the right to life, liberty and security of person.

Article 4: No one shall be held in slavery or servitude: slavery and the slave trade shall be prohibited in all their forms.

Article 5: No one shall be subjected to torture or to cruel, inhuman or degrading treatment or punishment.

Article 6: Everyone has the right to recognition everywhere as a person before the law.

Article 7: All are equal before the law and are entitled without any discrimination to equal protection of the law. All are entitled to equal protection against any discrimination in violation of this Declaration and against any incitement to such discrimination.

Article 8: Everyone has the right to an effective remedy by the competent national tribunals for acts violating the fundamental rights granted to him by the constitution or by law.

Article 9: No one shall be subjected to arbitrary arrest, detention and exile.

Article 10: Everyone is entitled in full equality to a fair and public hearing by an independent and impartial tribunal, in the determination of his rights and obligations and of any criminal charge against him.

Article 11: Everyone charged with a penal offence has the right to be presumed innocent until proved guilty according to law in a public trial at which he has had all the guarantees necessary for his defence.

No one shall be held guilty of any penal offence on account of any act or omission which did not constitute a penal offence, under national or international law, at the time when it was committed.

Nor shall a heavier penalty be imposed than the one that was applicable at the time the penal offence was committed.

Article 12: No one shall be subject to arbitrary interference with his privacy, family, home or correspondence, nor to attack upon his honour and reputation. Everyone has the right to the protection of the law against such interference of attacks.

Article 13: Everyone has the right to freedom of movement and residence within the border of each State. Everyone has the right to leave any country, including his own and to return to his country.

Article 14: Everyone has the right to seek and to enjoy in other countries asylum from persecution. The right may not be invoked in the case of prosecutions genuinely arising from non-political crimes or from acts contrary to purposes and principles of the United Nations.

Article 15: Everyone has the right to a nationality. No one shall be arbitrarily deprived of his nationality nor denied the right to change his nationality.

Article 16: Men and women of full age, without any limitation due to race, nationality or religion, have the right to marry and found a family. They are entitled to equal rights as to marriage, during marriage and at its dissolution. Marriage shall be entered into only with the free and full consent of the intending spouses. The family is the natural and fundamental group unit of society and is entitled to protection by society and the State.

Article 17: Everyone has the right to own property alone as well as in association with others.

No one shall be arbitrarily deprived of his property.

Article 18: Everyone has the right to freedom of thought, conscience and religion, this right includes freedom to change his religion or belief, and freedom, either alone or in community with others and in public or private to manifest his religion or belief in teaching, practice, worship and observance.

Article 19: Everyone has the right to freedom of opinion and expression, this right includes freedom to hold opinions without interference and to seek, receive and impart information and ideas through any media and regardless of frontiers.

Article 20: Everyone has the right to freedom of peaceful assembly and association. No one may be compelled to belong to an association.

Article 21: Everyone has the right to take part in the government of his country, directly or through freely chosen representatives. The will of the people shall be the basis of the authority of the government, this shall be expressed in periodic and genuine elections which shall be by universal and equal suffrage and shall be held by secret vote or by equivalent free voting procedures.

Articles 22 to 27 provide for economic, social and cultural rights. These rights are specified as an indispensable aspect of an individual's life, being necessary for one's dignity and personal development.

Article 22: Everyone, as a member of society, has the right to social security and is entitled to realization, through national effort and international cooperation and in accordance with the organization and resources of each State in the economic, social and cultural rights indispensable for his dignity and the free development of his personality.

Article 23: Everyone has the right to work, to free choice of employment, to just and favourable conditions of work and to protection against unemployment.

Everyone without any discrimination has the right to equal pay for equal work.

Everyone, who works has the right to just and favourable remuneration ensuring for himself and his family an existence of human dignity, and supplemented, if necessary by other means of social protection.

Everyone has the right to form and join trade unions for the protection of his interests.

Article 24: Everyone has the right to rest and leisure, including reasonable limitation of working hours and periodic holidays with pay.

Article 25: Everyone has a right to a standard of living adequate for the health and well-being of himself and of his family, including food, clothing, housing and medical care and necessary social service and the right to security in the event of unemployment, sickness, disability, widowhood, old age or lack of livelihood in circumstances beyond his control.

Motherhood and childhood are entitled to special care and assistance. All children, whether born in or out of wedlock shall enjoy the same social protection.

Article 26: Everyone has the right to education. Education shall be free at least in the elementary and fundamental stages. Elementary education shall be compulsory. Technical and professional education shall be made generally available and higher education shall be equally accessible to all on the basis of merit.

Education shall be directed to the full development of the human personality and to the strengthening of respect for human rights and fundamental freedoms. It shall promote understanding, tolerance and friendship among all nation, racial or religious groups, and shall further the activities of the United Nations for the maintenance of peace.

Parents have a prior right to choose the kind of education that shall be given to their children.

Article 27: Everyone has the right freely to participate in the cultural life of the community, to enjoy the arts and to share in scientific advancement and its benefits.

Everyone has the right to the protection of the moral and material interests resulting from any scientific, literary or artistic production of which he is the author.

Finally, **Articles 28, 29 and 30** establish a general framework to provide for the enjoyment of human rights: the recognition of the rightful social and international system that promotes human rights; a statement that humans have obligations to the community along with fundamental rights; and a reminder that no state or individual may utilize the Declaration to promote goals contrary to the mission or goals of the UN.

Article 28: Everyone is entitled to a social and international order in which the rights and freedoms set forth in this Declaration can be fully realized.

Article 29: Everyone has duties to the community in which alone the free and full development of his personality is possible.

In the exercise of his rights and freedoms, everyone shall be subject only to such limitations as are determined by law solely for the purpose of securing due recognition and respect for the rights and freedoms of others and of meeting the just requirements of morality, public order and the general welfare in a democratic society. These rights and freedoms may in no case be exercised contrary to the purposes and principles of the United Nations.

Article 30: Nothing in this Declaration may be interpreted as implying for any State, group or person any right to engage in any activity or to perform any act aimed at the destruction of any of the rights and freedoms set forth herein.

The UDHR is not a treaty. It, being a formal declaration does not have the force of law and is not legally enforceable. Its purpose, as highlighted in its Preamble, is to provide "a common understanding" of the human rights and fundamental freedoms referred to in the UN Charter and to serve "as a common standard of achievement for all peoples and all nations." Nevertheless, over the years, continuous reliance on this document for human rights interpretations has given it the status of customary international law. International organizations can hardly afford to ignore this declaration just because it lacks formal legal enforceability.

1.4 UN Covenants on Human Rights

Due to the highly generalized nature of the UDHR and the absence of legal sanctions it became imperative to draft out a more detailed list of rights along with its legal obligations. Towards this goal two instruments were drafted—(i) The International Covenant on Civil and Political Rights (ICCPR) embracing the traditional civil and political rights recognized in Western countries, and (ii) The International Covenant on Economic, Social and Cultural Rights (ICESCR) to fulfill the aspirations of socialist and Third World countries. Also, an (First) Optional Protocol to the International Covenant on Civil and Political Rights granted right to petition to the individual. The Covenants were adopted in 1966 and entered into force in 1976, almost a decade after their adoption. "While the provisions of the ICCPR were meant to be implemented *immediately* whereas those of the ICESCR were meant to be achieved *progressively* through long-range education, planning and promotion".[3]

Both the Covenants share a number of common substantive provisions. Article 1 (1) of both the Covenants proclaim that "all peoples have the right of self-determination". By virtue of that right they freely determine their political status and freely pursue their economic, social and cultural development. Each Covenant establishes a distinct international enforcement system designed to ensure that the State Parties comply with their obligations. Interestingly, the Optional Protocol provides scope for citizens to file petitions in cases of human rights violation, thus ensuring that human rights are truly internationalized.

International Covenant on Civil and Political Rights

The ICCPR enumerates an exhaustive list of rights under Articles 6-27 which are:

- Right to life
- Freedom from torture and inhuman treatment
- Freedom from slavery and forced labour
- Right to liberty and security
- Right of detained persons to be treated with humanity
- Freedom from imprisonment for debt
- Freedom of movement and of choice of residence
- Freedom of aliens from arbitrary expulsion
- Right to a fair trial
- Protection against ex-post facto law
- Right to recognition everywhere as a person before the law
- Right to privacy

- Freedom of thought, conscience and religion
- Freedom of speech and expression
- Prohibition of propaganda for war and of incitement to national, racial or religious hatred
- Right to peaceful assembly
- Freedom of association
- Right to marry and found a family
- Rights of child
- Right to vote, take part in public affairs
- Equality before law and equal protection of laws
- Rights of minorities to enjoy their own culture, religion and language

Apart from rights, the Covenant contains a "**derogation clause**" which permits the State Parties in times of public emergency that threatens the life of the nation to suspend all but seven (Articles 6, 7, 8, 11, 15, 16 and 18) of the most fundamental rights. Article 4 (2) of the Covenant lists the provisions from which no derogation is permitted. They are Article 6 (Right to life), Article 7 (prohibition of torture), Article 8 (prohibition of slavery), Article 11 (prohibition of imprisonment for non-fulfillment of contractual obligations), Article 15 (prohibition against retroactive criminal laws and penalties), Article 16 (right to be recognized as a person before the law), Article 18 (freedom of thought, conscience and religion). However, a state availing of the right of derogation should immediately inform other State Parties of the reasons for such derogation and the period till which such suspension shall remain in force. Moreover, right to derogation (1) must be strictly required by the exigencies of the situation; (2) they must not be in conflict with other international obligations; and (3) must not involve any discrimination based on race, colour, caste, sex, language, religion or social origin.

Basically, the purpose was to ensure that the State has the power to meet emergencies but again, suspension of rights should not be a regular affair and the Covenant allows derogation only in such emergencies that "threaten the life of the nation".

For the proper enforcement of rights, the Covenant established a Human Rights Committee and conferred on it various functions to ensure that the signatories comply with the obligations. These functions consist of the administration of the reporting system and the inter-state complaint mechanism provided for in the Covenant. The Committee consists of eighteen members who are nominated by State Parties but serve in their individual capacities and not as government representatives.

Administration of Reporting System: The Committee's main function is to examine reports of all State Parties regarding the measures adopted and progress made in the enjoyment of rights. Over the years, the committee has developed a comprehensive set of reporting guidelines and procedures for dealing with these reports. The guidelines are designed to ensure that the State Parties comply with the treaty obligations. Though, the Covenant does not expressly confer the right on the Committee to verify the state reports by undertaking investigations but it can seek permission from the States concerned to do so.

The evolution of the reporting system has accelerated in recent years, transforming it into an increasingly effective instrument for the implementation of the Covenant.

Inter-State Complaint Mechanism: The Covenant also provides for an inter-state complaint machinery that enables one State Party to charge another with violation of the treaty. Article 41 of the Covenant expressly states that a State Party to the present Covenant may at any time declare under this Article that it recognizes the competence of the Committee to receive and consider communications to the effect that a State Party claims that another State Party is not fulfilling its obligations under the present Covenant. The Covenant, further, lays down a special procedure for entertaining such complaints—

- If a State Party considers that another State Party is violating provisions of the Covenant, then it should bring it to the notice of the other State Party by a written communication.

- Within 3 months after the receipt of the communication, the receiving State shall give to the State which sent the communication, an explanation clarifying the matter with reference to the domestic procedures and remedies taken, pending or available in the matter.
- If the matter is not adjusted to the satisfaction of both State Parties concerned within six months after the receipt by the receiving State of the initial communication, either State shall have the right to refer the matter to the Committee, by notice given to the Committee and to the other State.
- The Committee shall deal with the matter only after it has ascertained that all the available domestic remedies have been invoked and exhausted, in conformity with the generally recognized principles of international law.
- The Committee shall offer its good offices to the State Parties for friendly solution of the matter.
- The Committee may call upon the State Parties concerned for supply of relevant information.
- The State Parties concerned shall have the right to be represented when the matter is being considered by the Committee and may make submissions orally or in writing.
- The Committee is under an obligation to submit its report within twelve months of the receipt of the notice.

International Covenant on Economic, Social and Cultural Rights

The Covenant lists out in detail the economic, social and cultural rights to be enjoyed by people and also lays down the steps that should be taken for its effective realization. Towards this end Article 2 of the present Covenant imposes an obligation upon State Parties to take steps individually and through international assistance and cooperation, especially economic and technical, subject to availability of resources, to achieve progressively the full realization of rights. Articles 6-15 provide rights as of:

- Right to work
- Right to just and favourable conditions of work including fair wages, equal pay for equal work and holidays with pay
- Right to form and join trade unions including the right to strike
- Right to social security
- Protection of the family including special assistance for mothers and children
- Right to an adequate standard of living, including adequate food, clothing and housing and the continuous improvement of living conditions
- Right to the highest attainable standard of physical and mental health
- Right to education with free and compulsory primary education and secondary and higher education made accessible to all
- Right to participate in cultural life and enjoy the benefits of scientific progress.

This Covenant does not establish any inter-state or individual complaint mechanism. But, to monitor the enforcement and implementation of the rights, State Parties to the ICSECR have to submit periodic reports to the Economic and Social Council on the measures adopted and progress made in the observance of rights contained therein. The Committee on Economic, Social and Cultural Rights, composed of 18 members has been created for reviewing state reports and making recommendations for better realisation of these rights.

1.5 Optional Protocols

The Optional Protocol to the International Covenant on Civil and Political Rights

This treaty, adopted as a separate instrument, emphasizes on the enforcement mechanism of the rights. It enables private individuals claiming to be victims of violation of the Covenant, to file "individual" communications or complaints with the Human Rights Committee. Before filing a complaint an individual should have exhausted all available domestic remedies. It should, however, be remembered that the complaints may only be filed against State Parties to the Covenant that have ratified the Protocol.

Second Optional Protocol to the International Covenant on Civil and Political Rights

This Protocol was adopted in the year 1989 and enforced in 1991. The basic objective of the Protocol is the abolition of death penalty, thereby contributing to the enhancement of human dignity and progressive development of human rights. Article 1 of the Second Optional Protocol states that—No one within the jurisdiction of a State Party shall be executed. Each State party shall take all necessary measures to abolish the death penalty within its jurisdiction. The *Second Optional Protocol to the International Covenant on Civil and Political Rights, aiming at the abolition of the death penalty*, adopted by the UN General Assembly in 1989, is of worldwide scope. It provides for the total abolition of the death penalty but allows state parties to retain the death penalty in time of war if they make a reservation to that effect at the time of ratifying or acceding to the Protocol. Any state which is a party to the International Covenant on Civil and Political Rights can become a party to the Protocol.

Optional Protocol to the International Covenant on Economic, Social and Cultural Rights

The Optional Protocol to the International Covenant on Economic, Social and Cultural Rights is an international treaty establishing complaint and inquiry mechanisms for the International Covenant on Economic, Social and Cultural Rights. It was adopted by the UN General Assembly on 10th December, 2008, and opened for signature on 24th September, 2009. The Optional Protocol establishes an individual complaints mechanism for the Covenant similar to those of the First Optional Protocol to the International

Covenant on Civil and Political Rights, Optional Protocol to the Convention on the Rights of Persons with Disabilities and Article 14 of the Convention on the Elimination of All Forms of Racial Discrimination. Parties agree to recognise the competence of the Committee on Economic, Social and Cultural Rights to consider complaints from individuals or groups who claim their rights under the Covenant have been violated. Complainants must have exhausted all available domestic remedies, and anonymous complaints and complaints referring to events which occurred before the country concerned joined the Optional Protocol are not permitted. The Committee can request information from and make recommendations to a party. Parties may also opt to permit the Committee to hear complaints from other parties, rather than just individuals.

The Protocol also includes an inquiry mechanism. Parties may permit the Committee to investigate report on and make recommendations on "grave or systematic violations" of the Convention. Parties may opt out of this obligation on signature or ratification.

The Optional Protocol requires ten ratifications to come into force.

1.6 Vienna Declaration and Programme of Action, 1993

The Vienna Declaration and Programme of Action were adopted on 25th June, 1993 by 171 States to strengthen the international communities' effort to promote and protect human rights. It was a concerted effort to strengthen the human rights protection machinery to better guarantee rights. It made concrete recommendations for strengthening and harmonizing the monitoring capacity of the United Nations system. It strongly recommended that State should be the best guarantor of human rights. Towards this end there is need for States and international organizations in cooperation with non-governmental organizations to create favourable conditions at the national, regional and local levels to ensure full and effective enjoyment of human rights.

The main features of the Declaration are as follows:

1. Human rights and fundamental freedoms are the birthright of all human beings; their promotion and protection is the first responsibility of Governments.
2. Effective international measures to guarantee and monitor the implementation of human rights standards should be taken in respect of people under foreign occupation, and effective legal protection against the violation of their human rights should be provided, in accordance with human rights norms and international law, particularly the Geneva Convention relating to the Protection of Civilian Persons in Time of war and other applicable norms of humanitarian law.
3. Democracy, development and respect for human rights and fundamental freedoms are interdependent and mutually reinforcing. Democracy is based on the freely expressed will of the people to determine their own political, economic, social and cultural systems and their full participation in all aspects of their lives. Therefore, promotion and protection of human rights at the national and international levels should be universal and unconditional.
4. Right to development is a universal and inalienable right. The right to development should be fulfilled so as to meet equitably the developmental and environmental needs of present and future generations. The World Conference on Human Rights recognizes that illicit dumping of toxic and dangerous substances and waste potentially constitutes a serious threat to the human rights to life and health of everyone.
5. The existence of widespread extreme poverty inhibits the full and effective enjoyment of human rights; its immediate alleviation and eventual elimination must remain a high priority for the international community.
6. The acts, methods and practices of terrorism in all its forms

and manifestations as well as linkage in some countries to drug trafficking are activities aimed at the destruction of human rights, fundamental freedoms and democracy, threatening territorial integrity, security of States and destabilizing legitimately constituted governments. The international community should take necessary steps to enhance cooperation to prevent and combat terrorism.

7. The human rights of women and of the girl child are an inalienable, integral part of universal human rights. Equal participation of women in political, economic, social, civil and cultural life at the national and international levels and the eradication of all forms of discrimination on grounds of sex are priority objectives of the international community.
8. The World Conference on Human Rights recognizes the inherent dignity and the unique contribution of indigenous to the plurality of society and strongly reaffirms the commitment of the international community to their economic, social and cultural well-being and their enjoyment of the fruits of sustainable development.
9. The Declaration also reaffirmed the right to seek and enjoy asylum from persecution as well as the right to return to one's own country.
10. Great importance must be given to the promotion and protection of the human rights of persons belonging to groups which have been rendered vulnerable, including migrant workers, the elimination of all forms of discrimination against them, and the strengthening and more effective implementation of existing human rights instruments.
11. Every State should provide an effective framework of remedies to redress human rights violations. The administration of justice including law enforcement and prosecutorial agencies and especially, an independent judiciary and legal profession in full conformity with applicable standards contained in international human

rights instruments, are essential to the full and no-discriminatory realization of human rights and indispensable to the processes of democracy and sustainable development.

The Vienna Declaration contains detailed implementation mechanism for minorities, indigenous peoples, women, children, migrant workers, and disabled people. It not only lays down principles of protection but emphasizes upon and obligation on the part of Governments to monitor safeguarding of rights.

1.7 Issue Specific UN Conventions and Treaties

Over the years, a large number of treaties have been adopted dealing with specific types of human rights violations as of discrimination against women, children, minorities, indigenous peoples. The major human rights treaties adopted by the UN are as follows:

- The Convention on the Prevention and Punishment of the Crime of Genocide
- International Convention on the Elimination of All Forms of Racial Discrimination
- International Convention on the Suppression and the Punishment of the Crime of Apartheid
- Convention on the Elimination of All Forms of Discrimination against Women
- Convention against Torture and Other Cruel, Inhuman or Degrading Treatment
- Convention on the Rights of the Child.

The Convention on the Prevention and Punishment of the Crime of Genocide

The Convention was adopted by the General Assembly in 1948 and it was enforced in 1951. The Convention defines "genocide" as the commission of certain enumerated acts "with intent to destroy, in whole or in part, a national, ethnic, racial or religious group, as such". It equivocally declares that genocide, whether committed in times of war or peace is a "crime under international law" and "persons committing genocide... shall be punished, whether they are constitutionally responsible rulers, public officials or private individuals". (Article IV)

International Convention on the Elimination of All Forms of Racial Discrimination

The Convention was adopted by the UN General Assembly in 1965 and entered into force in 1969. Any form of racial discrimination is prohibited by the treaty wherein it is defined as "any distinction, exclusion, restriction or preference based on race, colour, descent, or national or ethnic origin" having the purpose or effect of "nullifying or impairing the recognition, enjoyment or exercise, on an equal footing, of human rights and fundamental freedoms in the political, economic, social, cultural or any other field of public life". The State Parties to the Convention have the legal obligation to eliminate racial discrimination from their territory and enact legislations to ensure non-discrimination. The Convention establishes an enforcement mechanism through the Committee on the Elimination of Racial Discrimination (CERD). It has the responsibility of reviewing periodic reports submitted by State Parties as well as the power to deal with inter-state and individual communications. Besides the CERD, the Convention also confers jurisdiction on the International Court of Justice to deal with disputes between State Parties.

International Convention on the Suppression and the Punishment of the Crime of Apartheid

The Convention was adopted in 1973 but came into force in the year 1976. The Convention defines apartheid as policies of racial segregation and discrimination being practiced in 'Southern Africa'. It declares apartheid as a 'crime against humanity'. The Convention provides punishment not only to individuals, members of organizations and institutions but also to all those who directly abet, encourage or cooperate in its commission regardless where such individual is at the time of offence. In order to eliminate racial discrimination, a system of periodic reporting by State Parties has been instituted and a Group of Three constituted to review the reports. The UN Human Rights Commission has also been empowered to deal with such cases.

Convention on the Elimination of All Forms of Discrimination against Women

The CEDAW which seeks to eliminate discrimination against women was adopted by the UN General Assembly in 1979 and it came into force in 1981. The treaty specifies the nature of discrimination against women as "any distinction, exclusion or restriction made on the basis of sex" that impairs the enjoyment of women of "human rights and fundamental freedoms in the political, economic, social, cultural, civil or any other field". Furthermore State Parties are under an obligation to embody the principle of equality of men and women in the national constitutions and legislations. The Committee on Elimination of Discrimination against Women is under an obligation to review periodic reports submitted by State Parties regarding the measures adopted to give effect to the provisions of the treaty. It reports on its activities to the UN Commission on the Status of Women and the General Assembly.

Convention against Torture and Other Cruel, Inhuman or Degrading Treatment

This treaty was adopted by the UN General Assembly in 1984 and entered into force in 1987. The Convention attempts to prevent torture and other inhuman acts by public officials, individuals or groups. The treaty defines all acts of torture as offences under criminal law. The State Parties undertake to adopt "effective legislative, administrative, judicial or other measures to prevent torture under their territorial jurisdiction. Under the Convention, a Committee Against Torture (CAT) has been established which is responsible for implementing the terms of the treaty. The Committee has the right to initiate inquiry on the basis of reliable information of infliction of torture by a State Party. It also receives periodic reports as well as inter-State and individual complaints mechanism.

Convention on the Rights of the Child

The treaty seeking to accord children with social, civil, political, economic and cultural rights was adopted by the UN General Assembly in 1989 and it entered into force in 1990. This is the first time that children were regarded as subjects of international rights. The Convention seeks to protect children against dangerous practices and exploitation, abuse and illegal trafficking. Moreover, the Convention establishes a Committee on the Rights of the Child to examine the progress made by State Parties concerning child welfare and also to review periodic reports submitted by State Parties in the implementation of the treaty.

1.8 Human Rights and Duties: The Linkage

Since the end of the Second World War, the world has witnessed the renewal, amplification of rights as a major concern in politics, as a pivot of popular political mobilization, and a popular agenda of political deliberations. This has led to an exaltation of the notion of rights to the utter disregard to duties and responsibilities. However, it cannot be denied that a just moral order presupposes the existence of a set of duties and responsibilities to be followed by all. The recent shift in the perspective of rights as correlative of duties has brought about a renewed importance of duties in recent social science literature.

A duty, in literal terms, signifies what we ought to do and what we ought not. It entails a set of binding obligations on the part of individual and groups towards family, society, state and to the larger community of nations. A person cannot have rights without having duties, and only realizing his own duties equally with rights it is possible to obtain real freedom, justice and peace in the world.

The American Declaration of the Rights and Duties of Man, adopted in 1948 by the Organisation of American States, declares in its Preamble: *Rights and duties are interrelated in every social and political activity of man. While rights exalt individual liberty, duties express the dignity of that liberty. Duties of a juridical nature presuppose others of a moral nature which support them in principle and constitute their basis.*

Emphasizing the correlation of rights with duties, the Universal Declaration of Human Rights, proclaims the duty to respect the rights of others (Article 29 of Universal Declaration of Human Rights, 1948).

Article 29 (1) of the UDHR provides that everyone has duties to the community in which alone the free and full development of his personality is possible.

Article 29 (2) In the exercise of his rights and freedoms, everyone shall be subject only to such limitations as are determined by law solely for the purpose of securing due recognition and respect for the rights and freedoms of others and of meeting the just requirements of morality, public order and the general welfare in a democratic society.

The emphasis on duties in the Declaration of Rights implies that for the observance and enjoyment of rights, fulfillment of responsibilities is necessary. Rights require an environment where individual can be at his best and this environment can be guaranteed if everyone fulfills the duties assigned to him.

1.9 Declaration on the Right and Responsibility of Individuals, Groups and Organs of Society to Promote and Protect Universally Recognised Human Rights and Fundamental Freedoms, 1999

On the basis of Article 29 of the Universal Declaration of Human Rights, the Declaration of the Rights and Responsibilities of Individuals in 1999. It categorically emphasizes individuals by dint of good breeding and education, and by using their intellect and consciousness work toward creation of feelings of brotherhood, solidarity and reasonable co-operation.

- ***Duties of states***

Article 2

1. Each State has a prime responsibility and duty to protect, promote and implement all human rights and fundamental freedoms, *inter alia*, by adopting such steps as may be necessary to create all conditions necessary in the social, economic, political and other fields, as well as the legal guarantees required to ensure that all persons under its jurisdiction, individually and in association with others, are able to enjoy all those rights and freedoms in practice.
2. Each State shall adopt such legislative, administrative and other steps as may be necessary to ensure that the rights and freedoms referred to in the present Declaration are effectively guaranteed.

Article 3

Domestic law consistent with the Charter of the United Nations and other international obligations of the State in the field of human rights and fundamental freedoms is the juridical framework within which human rights and fundamental freedoms should be implemented and enjoyed and within which all activities referred to in the present Declaration for the promotion, protection and effective realization of those rights and freedoms should be conducted.

Article 14

1. The State has the responsibility to take legislative, judicial, administrative or other appropriate measures to promote the understanding by all persons under its jurisdiction of their civil, political, economic, social and cultural rights.
2. Such measures shall include, *inter alia*:
   (*a*) The publication and widespread availability of national laws and regulations and of applicable basic international human rights instruments;

(*b*) Full and equal access to international documents in the field of human rights, including the periodic reports by the State to the bodies established by the international human rights treaties to which it is a party, as well as the summary records of discussions and the official reports of these bodies.

3. The State shall ensure and support, where appropriate, the creation and development of further independent national institutions for the promotion and protection of human rights and fundamental freedoms in all territory under its jurisdiction, whether they be ombudsmen, human rights commissions or any other form of national institution.

Article 15

The State has the responsibility to promote and facilitate the teaching of human rights and fundamental freedoms at all levels of education and to ensure that all those responsible for training lawyers, law enforcement officers, the personnel of the armed forces and public officials include appropriate elements of human rights teaching in their training programme.

- ***Duties of individuals/groups/organizations***

Article 16

Individuals, non-governmental organizations and relevant institutions have an important role to play in contributing to making the public more aware of questions relating to all human rights and fundamental freedoms through activities such as education, training and research in these areas to strengthen further, *inter alia*, understanding, tolerance, peace and friendly relations among nations and among all racial and religious groups, bearing in mind the various backgrounds of the societies and communities in which they carry out their activities

Article 18

1. Everyone has duties towards and within the community, in which alone the free and full development of his or her personality is possible.
2. Individuals, groups, institutions and non-governmental organizations have an important role to play and a responsibility in safeguarding democracy, promoting human rights and fundamental freedoms and contributing to the promotion and advancement of democratic societies, institutions and processes.
3. Individuals, groups, institutions and non-governmental organizations also have an important role and a responsibility in contributing, as appropriate, to the promotion of the right of everyone to a social and international order in which the rights and freedoms set forth in the Universal Declaration of Human Rights and other human rights instruments can be fully realized.

The 1999 Declaration seems to clearly delineate rights and responsibilities for all in society—a universal code of ethical obligations. This would rectify the present imbalance of more emphasis on rights. Demands for human rights are portrayed as leading to a selfish individualism, where the individual makes demands on the community but offers nothing in return. According to one eminent group of former world leaders, "exclusive insistence on rights can lead to endless dispute and conflict. Only by emphasizing human responsibilities can we move from the "freedom of indifference to the freedom of involvement".[4]

While the earlier Declarations on duties did not provide for any mechanism to enforce duties, Article 39 of the 1999 Declaration enunciates the duty and responsibility, primarily of the States, to provide for and enforce effective national judicial, administrative, legislative remedies. Furthermore, establishment of tripartite councils composed of State, civil society and private sector representatives in cooperation with States, relevant civil society organizations, national, regional and international intergovernmental organizations/commissions have been proposed for better protection of rights and duties. It may be concluded that it is not enough to have ethical guidelines to perform duties; to create a healthy human rights environment requires sincere performance of one's duties towards others, community, society, country and the larger community of nations and this alone can prevent the clash of civilizations.

Notes

1. M.P. Dube, *Perspectives on Human Rights*, in M.P. Dube and Neeta Bora, (eds.), Perspectives on Human Rights, Anamika Publishers and Distributors Pvt. Limited, New Delhi, 2000, p. 10.
2. *http://www.hrea.org/lib*
3. A.P.Vijapur, *The Universal Declaration of Human Rights—A Cornerstone of Modern Human Rights Regime*, in A.P.Vijapur and Kumar Suresh, (ed.), Perspectives on Human Rights, Manak Publications, New Delhi, 1999, p. 13.
4. Introductory Comment to A *Universal Declaration of Human Responsibilities*, published by the Inter Action Council, 1 September 1997, p.1, www.ichrp.org/files/reports/10/103_report_en.pdf

2

Promotion of Human Rights : International Mechanisms

Since 1945 promotion and protection of human rights has been a major preoccupation for the United Nations. The horrors of the Second World War have strengthened the resolve that respect for human rights and human dignity "is the foundation of freedom, justice and peace in the world". Over the years, a whole network of human rights instruments and mechanisms have been developed by the United Nations to ensure the primacy of human rights and to confront human rights violations wherever they occur. In addition, all states have an obligation to promote respect for human rights standards by introducing mechanisms within their political systems as well as contribute to constructive dialogue through international forums.

The UN's system of human rights protection has three main components:

- it establishes international standards through its Charter, treaties, declarations, agreements, and documents;
- it mandates Special Rapporteurs and experts, committees and treaty bodies, to work for the promotion and protection of human rights;
- it offers technical expertise through the Voluntary Fund for Advisory Services and Technical Assistance in the field of Human Rights.

2.1 UN and Its Organs

Since inception the United Nations have been continuously striving "to reaffirm faith in fundamental human rights, in the dignity and worth of the human persons, in the equal rights of men and women and of nations, large and small" and to achieve this purpose is authorized to take appropriate measures. The UN Charter contains a number of provisions for setting standards for human rights protection and promotion. Article 13 states that the General Assembly shall initiate studies and make recommendations for the purpose of promoting international co-operation in the economic, social, cultural, educational and health fields, and assisting in the realization of human rights and fundamental freedoms for all without distinction as to race, sex, language or religion. Furthermore, Article 62 states that the Economic and Social Council may make recommendations for the purpose of promoting respect for, and observance of, human rights and fundamental freedoms for all without distinction as to race, sex, language or religion. Under Article 64, the ECOSOC may make arrangements with the Members of the United Nations and with the specialized agencies to obtain reports on the steps taken to give effect to its own recommendations and make communicate its observations on these reports to the General Assembly.

The **General Assembly** essentially performs deliberative, supervisory functions. Article 13 of the Charter provides that the General Assembly shall initiate studies and make recommendations for the purpose of assisting in the realization of human rights and fundamental freedoms for all without distinction as to race, sex, language or religion. The **Security Council** is empowered by the Charter to take appropriate measures, including action aimed at the pacific settlement of disputes and preventive and enforcement action. Specifically in matters concerning human rights it is the **Economic and Social Council** which plays a substantial role. It initiates studies and reports with regard to international economic, social, cultural, educational, health and related matters. It prepares draft conventions on specific issues and submits them to the General Assembly. In addition, the Council is responsible for coordinating the activities of the specialized agencies through consultation with, and recommendations to, those agencies and through recommendations to the General Assembly. At times it also makes recommendations to inter-governmental and non-governmental organizations as well as individuals and groups.

2.2 UN Charter Based Mechanisms

The type of protection provided by the United Nations on issues of human rights is based on either Charter-based or Treaty-based mechanisms. Those mechanisms based on the UN Charter include: **the Universal Declaration of Human Rights** (discussed in detail in Chapter1); **the Commission on Human Rights; and the Sub-Commission on the Promotion and Protection of Human Rights.**

Commission on Human Rights

The Commission on Human Rights is a Charter-based body dealing directly with human rights. It is assisted by the Sub-Commission on the Promotion and Protection of Human Rights, individual experts, representatives, and Special Rapporteurs. The Commission on Human Rights meets for six weeks each year in Geneva, although it may also meet in majority-endorsed "Special Sessions" in order to provide the most expeditious manner of dealing with human rights abuses. From its inception, the Commission has influenced international human rights standards. In fact, it played a significant part in the drafting of the Universal Declaration of Human Rights in 1948. Since then, it has formed standards relating to the right to development, civil and political rights, economic, social and cultural rights, elimination of racial discrimination, torture, the rights of the child and the rights of human rights defenders.

One of the major functions of the Commission is monitoring the implementation of human rights standards set forth by it. It may turn to any number of permanent or special procedures when examining a specific area of human rights. Its two permanent procedures are the 1503 Procedure and the 1235 Procedure; its special procedures include fact-finding missions, thematic mechanisms and advisory services.

The **1503 Procedure** is a confidential procedure named after ECOSOC Resolution 1503 by which it was established. It becomes operative when the Commission receives a communication about a consistent pattern of gross human rights violations. Violations considered under this procedure include genocide, apartheid, ethnic discrimination, torture, forced mass migrations and mass imprisonment without a trial. The report of consistent gross human rights violations to the Commission may not be an anonymous one, yet does not require the consent of the state concerned for an investigation to take place. This regulation enables the Commission in deciding how to deal a situation. Following its investigation, the Commission then decides the course of action. When a 1503 Procedure has failed to stop a human rights violation it has investigated, the Commission on Human Rights may invoke the **1235 Procedure** under which it can hold an annual public debate about the gross violations of human rights in question. If this also fails to adequately affect the situation, the Commission may move to have ECOSOC pass a resolution condemning the violators. This public condemnation undermines the legitimacy of the government.

Among the special procedures available to the Commission on Human Rights, **fact-finding missions** are a useful tool. In a fact-finding mission, group of experts studies a human rights situation and looks for violations in a given state with the purpose of gathering information for a 1503 or a 1235 procedure. However, a fact-finding mission may only occur with the consent of the state whose human rights record is being questioned.

Another special procedure available to the Commission on Human Rights is a **thematic mechanism** or mandate. Working groups and/or Special Rapporteurs investigate human rights violations and the problems they have caused on a multi-state level.

Lastly, the Commission on Human Rights offers **advisory services** to nations that request it. The Commission provides educational and informational assistance to states in order to help them observe a high level of human rights protection.

Sub-Commission on Human Rights

The Sub-Commission was established by the Commission on Human Rights at its first meeting in 1947, and was titled the Sub-Commission on Prevention of Discrimination and Protection of Minorities before a 1999 vote to change its name. It serves as the main subsidiary body to the Commission on Human Rights.

The Sub-Commission is comprised of 26 member experts acting independently, without affiliation to their state of origin, though they are elected by the Commission proportionally according to geographical population distribution. "Presently, member experts are divided as follows: seven from Africa, six from Western Europe and other States, five from Asia, five from Latin America and three from Eastern Europe. Each member has one alternate; half the members and their alternates are elected every two years and each serves for a term of four years."[1] The Sub-Commission meets for three weeks each year in Geneva; government officials, staff of UN Specialized agencies and NGO observers may also attend their meetings.

The Sub-Commission's task is to undertake studies and make recommendations to the Commission on Human Rights concerning the prevention of discrimination of any kind relating to human rights and fundamental freedoms and the protection of racial, national, religious and linguistic minorities.

Office of the High Commissioner for Human Rights

The position of the High Commissioner for Human Rights was established by the General Assembly of the United Nations in December 1993. The Commissioner holds the principal position of promoting human rights and dealing with human rights activities in the UN, and must also maintain dialogue with all member states on the subject of human rights. The major responsibilities of the High Commissioner include: crisis management; prevention and early warning of abuses; assistance to states in periods of political transition; promotion of substantive rights to governments; and coordination and rationalization of human rights programmes.

2.3 Treaty Based Mechanisms

Unlike the UDHR, the various treaties signed by state parties create binding obligations to promote human rights protection within their national frontiers as well as regularly report on the measures taken for the same. All these treaties are based on principles of non-discrimination, justice, equality and implementation of the provisions is the singular objective of the treaties.

The following treaty bodies, composed of experts serving in their personal capacity, were established to monitor compliance with United Nations human rights instruments:

- The Committee on the Elimination of Racial Discrimination (CERD) monitors the implementation of the International Convention on the Elimination of All Forms of Racial Discrimination since 1969.
- The Committee on the Elimination of Discrimination Against Women (CEDAW), monitors the implementation of the International Convention on the Elimination of All Forms of Discrimination against Women since 1982.
- The Committee on the Rights of the Child (CRC) monitors the implementation of the Convention on the Rights of the Child since 1990 as well as two Optional Protocols to the CRC on child soldiers and child exploitation.
- The Committee Against Torture (CAT) monitors the implementation of the Convention Against Torture and Other Cruel, Inhuman or Degrading Treatment or Punishment since 1987.
- The Human Rights Committee (HRC) monitors implementation of the Covenant on Civil and Political Rights since 1976.
- The Committee on Economic, Social and Cultural Rights (CESCR) oversees implementation of the Covenant on Economic, Social and Cultural Rights since 1987.
- The Committee on Migrant Workers (CMW) monitors implementation of the International Convention on the

Protection of the Rights of all Migrant Workers and Members of their Families since 2004.

- The Committee on Enforced Disappearance (CED) monitors implementation of the International Convention for the Protection of All Persons from Enforced Disappearance since 2010.
- The Committee on the Rights of Persons with Disabilities (CRPD) monitors implementation of the International Convention on the Rights of Persons with Disabilities since 2008.

It should be noted that these Committees are established under the respective instruments, with members elected by the States parties, with the exception of the Committee on Economic, Social and Cultural Rights, whose membership is elected by Economic and Social Council. Each of these bodies are composed of independent experts who examine the reports that signatory nations submit under the treaty. These committees are also in charge of issuing concluding observations, where they summarize their concerns and also give recommendations for the future.

2.4 UN Human Rights Advisory Services

The United Nations advisory services programme began in 1955, providing institution-building assistance and other help to Member States at their request. In 1987, the Secretary-General established the Voluntary Fund for Advisory Services and Technical Assistance in Human Rights. Over the last few years, the United Nations Centre for Human Rights and Electoral Assistance Division have been continuously working to provide technical assistance in the following areas for a better human rights environment:

Reforming national laws: Incorporation of international human rights norms into national laws and constitutions is a key element in the protection of human rights. Assistance in drafting new constitutions and laws in line with human rights conventions has been provided to, *inter alia,* Bulgaria, Malawi, Mongolia and Nepal.

Supporting democratization and advising on electoral procedures: A just and democratic environment is the basis of a rights friendly system and to further this objective assistance has been provided to several countries on holding elections and setting up national human rights institutions.

Assisting in the drafting of national laws and preparation of national reports: Regional and sub-regional training courses have been held in Africa, Latin America and Asia and the Pacific for incorporation of different human rights standards in the laws and policies of the member countries.

Strengthening national and regional institutions: Assistance has been provided to institutions in various countries to strengthen human rights protection and promotion activities.

Training criminal justice personnel—judges, lawyers, prosecutors and police: State parties are encouraged to spread awareness among the citizenry through various conferences, seminars, courses, workshops, fellowships, scholarships, the provision of information and documentation. Lawyers and police are regularly trained to prevent violation of human rights of under-trials and prisoners.

Despite creation of so many mechanisms, gross violations continue to occur in most parts of the world. Uniform application of human rights monitoring standards may not yield the same results everywhere. It should be accepted that since conditions vary from country to country and region to region, it is important for the States to develop their own ideas for constructive reforms to improve the effectiveness of the UN treaty monitoring system. In consonance with the treaties and UN institutions, government departments, national human rights institutions, media and civil society should take necessary initiative to carry the agenda forward.

Note

1. http://www.ch/html/menu2/sc.htm

3

Promotion of Human Rights: Regional Mechanisms

Since its formation the United Nations has been involved consistently in the promotion and protection of human rights. However, as a single body it is practically impossible to look into the intricate matters of human rights violations in each and every region of the world. Regional organizations have, therefore, taken the initiative to establish institutional mechanisms to promote awareness of human rights. Regional human rights systems are able to better address a wide variety of human rights issues in smaller states.

3.1 The European Commission

Europe, at the end of the war suffered much devastation in terms of massive social and economic problems, widespread atrocities, racism. To renew efforts of peacekeeping and cooperation with one another after the war ended, leaders throughout the region founded three organizations: the Council of Europe, the European Union (formerly the European Coal and Steel Community), and later, the Organization for Security and Cooperation in Europe (formerly the Conference on Security and Cooperation in Europe). These organizations have survived the Cold War and the fall of Communism, and continue to this day to serve as forums for dialogue among member-states for furtherance of treaty objectives.

Instruments for Protection of Human Rights

The Council of Europe, a regional inter-governmental organization, established in 1949 has made and continues to make fervent efforts to promote human rights:

3.2.1 Convention for the Protection of Human Rights and Fundamental Freedoms

The Convention for the Protection of Human Rights and Fundamental Freedoms, known simply as the European Convention on Human Rights (ECHR), was the Council of Europe's first legal treaty to protect human rights, as well as the first international human rights treaty with enforceable mechanisms. Based primarily on the UDHR, it was signed in Rome on November 4, 1950, and entered into force on September 3, 1953. Only member states of the COE can become a party to the ECHR.

The ECHR's preamble, guided by the UDHR provides for "the maintenance and further realization of human rights and fundamental freedoms," which "are the foundation of justice and peace in the world and are best maintained on the one hand by an effective political democracy and on the other by a common understanding and observance of the human rights upon which they depend."

The essential features of the system are:

- a list of fundamental rights and freedoms;
- an obligation on member states to secure these rights and freedoms for all the people in their territory;
- a system for enforcement and remedies based on a Court of Human Rights whose decisions should be accepted by member states: failure to accept the decision can lead to political or diplomatic pressure from the Committee of Ministers;
- a special 'right of individual petition' by individuals against their own government.

The treaty mainly deals with civil and political rights, which are found in articles 1-18 as of the right to life (Article 2); the right not to suffer torture or inhuman or degrading treatment or punishment (Article 3); the right not to suffer slavery or forced labour (Article 4); the right to liberty and security (Article 5); the right to a fair trial (Article 6); the right not to be punished other than on the basis of law (Article 7); the right to respect for private and family life, home and correspondence (Article 8); the right to freedom of thought, conscience and religion (Article 9); the right to freedom of expression (Article 10); the right to freedom of assembly and association (Article 11); the right to marry (Article 12). Articles 19-51 list the working mechanisms of the European Court and Commission, while Protocol 1, 4, 7, 12 and 13 include additional rights.[1] The right of individual complaint (article 25) obliges the states to accept the Court as having authority to rule over issues from within that state.

3.2.2 European Court of Human Rights

Originally the Convention established two institutions: European Commission of Human Rights and European Court of Human Rights. The synchronization between the two institutions initially worked well since the Court dealt with a relatively small caseload. However, the caseload facing the court grew from 16 cases between 1960 and 1975 to 119 cases in 1997 alone. On 1st November, 1998, Protocol 11 of the European Convention on Human Rights came into force, eliminating the Commission of Human Rights as a new European Court of Human Rights and replacing the former system.

European Court of Human Rights was established with the ECHR on 3rd September, 1953. It has jurisdiction over COE member states that have opted to accept the Court's optional jurisdiction. Once a state has done so, all Court decisions regarding it are binding. Judges are elected to the Court by the Council of Europe's Parliamentary Assembly.

The principal function of the Court is to declare whether or not, in particular cases, there has been a violation of the Convention. Virtually all the cases brought before it are from individuals bringing cases in their own interest against their own state.

- The Court receives an application from the person who alleges they are a victim of a violation or from the state that alleges a violation by another state.
- It considers whether or not the case is admissible (before 1998 this was done by the Commission).
- If a case is admissible, the Court can then seek further details and receive further submissions from the parties.
- The Court makes a judgment on whether there has been a violation of the Convention. If so, it rules on whether the finding of a violation is a sufficient remedy or whether damages, 'just satisfaction', should be paid by the state involved and whether the state should also pay the applicant's costs.
- The Court submits its findings, on whether there has been a violation and what the remedy should be, to the Committee of Ministers which has the responsibility to supervise the judgment and ensure it is put into effect by the government of the state involved.
- Apart from these conventional functions, the Court can also render advice, when asked for, on the interpretation of the terms of the treaty.

The Court accepts applications of instances of human rights violations from individuals as well as states. However, it is rare for a state to submit allegations against another state, unless the violation is severe. In order for an application to be accepted by the Court, all domestic legal remedies available to the applicant must have been exhausted. Additionally:

- A non-anonymous petitioner must bring the case to the Court within six months of the final domestic ruling on it.
- The issue must be a violation of a guarantee set forth in the European Convention.
- The applicant must be a "victim." (However, terms specify that one does not have to have been directly persecuted to be considered a victim.)

- Petitioners may not repeat the substance of a previous petition.

The Court then holds a public hearing to determine if there has been a violation to the Convention. The Court normally sits as a Chamber of nine judges, including one from the country in question, but in rare instances can seat a Grand Chamber consisting of 21 judges. If the application is declared *admissible*, the Court usually advocates reaching a friendly settlement, which ranges from a change in the law to compensation.

European Commission on Human Rights

Although the European Commission on Human Rights became obsolete in 1998 with the restructuring of the Court of Human Rights, it held an important role in assisting the European Court of Human Rights from 1953 to 1998. Commission members were elected by the Committee of Ministers and would hold office for six years (during which time they were to act independently, without allegiance to any state). Their role was to consider if a petition was admissible to the Court. If so, the Commission would examine the petition to determine the facts of the case and look for parties that could help settle the case in a friendly manner. If a friendly settlement could not take place, the Commission would issue a report on the established facts with an opinion on whether or not a violation had occurred.

In addition, a number of treaties have been signed for better promotion of human rights.

European Social Charter

The European Social Charter, adopted in 1961 and monitored by the European Committee of Social Rights, guarantees economic, social and cultural rights, such as the rights to housing, health, education, employment, social protection, movement of persons, and non-discrimination. A new version of the Charter (revised in 1996) came into force in 1999.

European Committee of Social Rights

The European Committee of Social Rights (ECSR) is composed of independent experts serving six-year terms that are renewable for one term. States must submit annual reports of how they have followed the standards laid out in the Charter. The Committee reviews the annual reports submitted by States and then publishes decisions known as "Conclusions." If a state ignores a Conclusion of a violation, the Committee of Ministers addresses the state, asking it to rectify the problem, either by changing a law or a practice (or both).

European Convention for the Prevention of Torture and Inhuman or Degrading Treatment or Punishment

The European Convention for the Prevention of Torture was adopted in 1987 and entered into force in 1989 and was amended by Protocol 1 and 2. The Convention created the European Committee for the Prevention of Torture, to monitor the treaty.

Committee for the Prevention of Torture

The Committee for the Prevention of Torture (CPT) monitors the European Convention for the Prevention of Torture and Inhuman or Degrading Treatment or Punishment. It is composed of independent, impartial experts who serve four-year terms and may be re-elected twice; there is one member per signatory state.

The CPT visits places of detention, such as prisons, detention centers, police stations and mental health and elderly care institutions, with delegations of two or more members to monitor treatment of those being held. The CPT writes a report on countries it visits. In the reports, the CPT makes recommendations to ensure prevention of torture and ill-treatment. Governments must then respond to the recommendations. On rare occasions, the CPT may make a public statement should a state fail to incorporate the CPT's recommendations. However, recommendations are generally kept confidential.

Framework Convention for the Protection of National Minorities

The Framework Convention for the Protection of National Minorities, the first binding international treaty to offer protection specifically for minorities, was adopted in 1995 and entered into force in February 1998. Its Preamble discusses the need to protect national minorities, in the context of the disintegration and enmity of the central and eastern European states of the former Eastern bloc. The Preamble states, "A pluralist and genuinely democratic society should not only respect the ethnic, cultural, linguistic and religious identity of each person belonging to a national minority, but also create appropriate conditions enabling them to express, preserve and develop this identity." The Framework Convention is monitored by the Committee of Ministers, which is assisted by an Advisory Committee of independent experts.

European Commission against Racism and Intolerance (ECRI)

The European Commission against Racism and Intolerance was set up in 1993 to fight racism (the belief that certain races are inferior), xenophobia (fear of foreigners), anti-Semitism (prejudice against Jews), and other forms of intolerance. The Commission has one member per COE member state. Members are appointed by governments, although they serve independently.

Commissioner for Human Rights

The Commissioner for Human Rights was established in 1999 to perform three main duties:

1. Promoting human rights education and awareness of human rights;
2. Identifying areas of laws that fail to recognize human rights to a full extent;
3. Promoting respect for and enjoyment of human rights in COE member states.

4.2 The Inter-American Human Rights System

The Organization of American States (OAS), created under the Charter of the Organization of American States establishes two main institutions designed specifically for human rights protection and promotion: *the Inter-American Commission on Human Rights and the Inter-American Court of Human Rights.* The purpose of these two institutions is to further democracy through increased participation of the civil society in governance and strengthening of rule of law as well as addressing specific issues pertaining to women, children, communities, environment and labourers.

The Inter-American Commission is the principal institution created for protection and promotion of human rights. It is based in Washington DC (USA) and is composed of seven independent experts who are elected to four year terms by the OAS General Assembly. During its sessions, it hears from individuals and representatives from organizations on various claims of human rights abuses. The main duty of the Commission on Human Rights is to hear and oversee petitions that have been made against a member state of the OAS claiming a human rights abuse. The human rights universally protected by the Commission, are those found in the American Declaration of the Rights and Duties of Man.

Any individual, group of people, or NGO who are legally recognized in at least one OAS member state may file a petition; the petition may be submitted by either the victim or a third party may do so, with or without the victim's knowledge. There are two types of petitions that may be filed: either a general petition or a collective petition:

- A general petition is filed when a widespread form of human rights violations that is not limited to just one group of people or just one incident has occurred.
- A collective petition is filed when there are numerous victims of a specific incident violating human rights.

All petitions must include the name, nationality, profession or occupation, postal address, and signature of the person submitting the petition. All petitions filed must include certain facts to be admissible. Petitions should state the place where the violation occurred, the date on which it happened, the names of the victims, and the names of state officials involved with the violation. Another useful inclusion to a petition is a list of the rights violated. These petitions, which may be based on either civil and political rights or social, economic, and cultural rights, may refer to OAS human rights documents, as well as human rights documents from the United Nations or other regional bodies. They may also refer to precedents set by the Inter-American Commission on Human Rights or the Inter-American Court of Human Rights.

Eligibility of a petition depends on a few further criterions. Petitions, similar to the European system, would be acceptable only when all available domestic remedies have been exhausted. If the petitioner cannot prove this, the state's government may be asked to do so, and if the state can show that some domestic legal opportunities are still available to the petitioner, then the petitioner must demonstrate that one of four situations applies: either access to these remedies has been denied or prevented, there has been an unnecessary delay in judgment, there was a denial of adequate legal counsel, or the domestic legislation does not provide due process to protect the rights violated.

The petition must be filed within six months of the final ruling. Extensions are granted when the state interfered with the process, and then the petition must be filed within a reasonable amount of time. The government's response is then forwarded to the petitioner, who has thirty days to comment on the response as well as submit further material, if desired. The Commission then will decide whether or not to hold the oral hearing; it is authorized but not obligated to do so. The petitioner may also request for the Commission to undertake an on-site investigation in the country in question. The Commission will only investigate for allegations of widespread human rights violations within a country, and look at individual cases then as demonstrative of a broader theme. This method is rarely undertaken for just an individual case.

The Commission, after making its decision on the petition, releases judgment on what should be done by issuing recommendations to the state concerned. In the event that the state is party to the American Convention, the Commission must attempt to formulate a friendly settlement, if possible. If a friendly settlement is either not sought or reached, the Commission writes a report with the facts of the case and the Commission's conclusions, recommendations, and proposals. The state concerned and the Commission then have 3 months to decide whether or not to submit the case to the Court of Human Rights or settle the matter. Next, the Commission formally adopts an opinion and a conclusion with time limits for the government to undertake the proposed measures.

States that are not parties to the Convention are not subject to the friendly settlement clause. In that situation, the Commission will undergo its fact finding and then determine the merits of the petition, adopt a final decision (usually a lengthy resolution) with recommendations and deadlines.

In addition to investigating cases, the Commission may, on its own initiative, investigate and issue a report on the human rights situation in any OAS member state. The Commission bases its independent studies on reports it has received from NGOs and individuals. The Commission also submits an annual report to the OAS General Assembly, with information on resolutions of particular cases, reports on human rights situation in various states, and discussions of areas needing further action to promote and protect human rights.

Inter-American Court of Human Rights

The Inter-American Court of Human Rights was established in 1978 with the entry into force of the American Convention. It is composed of seven judges who are nominated and elected for a six year term by the parties to the American Convention; a justice may be re-elected only once. The Court has its permanent seat in San José (Costa Rica).

The Court's jurisdiction is limited. It may only hear cases where the state involved has

(a) ratified the American Convention on Human Rights,
(b) has accepted the Court's optional jurisdiction (as of 1992, only 13 of 35 nations had signed this optional jurisdiction),
(c) the Inter-American Commission on Human Rights has completed its investigation, and
(d) the case was referred to the Court either by the Commission or the state involved in the case within three months of the release of the Commission's report. An individual or a petitioner may not independently bring forth a case to be considered by the Court.

In the event that the Commission brings a case forward to the Court of Human Rights, it notifies the original petitioner. At this point, the petitioner or an attorney has the opportunity to request necessary measures, including precautions for witnesses and protections for evidence.

The Court's deliberations are always secret and confidential; its judgments and opinions are published. If the Court rules that a right has been violated, it will order that the situation be rectified. It may award compensation to the victim for actual damage but it will not award punitive damages.

Human Rights Treaties and Declarations

Since its inception, the OAS has adopted several declarations and treaties relating to human rights:

1. American Convention on Human Rights (1969)[2]

This treaty, which was adopted in 1969 and entered into force in 1978, enforces much of the notions contained in the American Declaration of the Rights and Duties of Man. As a treaty, it is binding only on the nations that have signed it. It focuses mainly on civil and political human rights, and offers more detailed definitions of these rights than the Declaration does. The treaty also created the Inter-American Court of Human Rights. It offered signatories a chance to sign on to an additional protocol to accept the Court's jurisdiction.

Like the Declaration, the Convention contains a "general limitation clause", stating that the rights of each person are necessarily limited by the rights of others, by the security of all, and by the just demands of the general welfare in a democratic society. The Convention also lists additional justifiable reasons for restricting rights, including: national security, public safety, public order, public health or morals, and the rights or freedoms of others. Additionally, Article 27 permits the suspension of some rights during a national emergency.

2. Cartagena Declaration on Refugees (1984)[3]

In 1984, ten Latin American states adopted the Cartagena Declaration on Refugees which contained an extension of the refugee definition found in the 1951 UN Refugee Convention. "...persons who have fled their country because their lives, safety, or freedom have threatened by generalised violence, foreign aggression, internal conflicts, massive violations of human rights or other circumstances which have seriously disturbed pubic order." This definition was approved by the 1985 General Assembly of the OAS, which resolved to urge member states to extend support and implement the conclusions and recommendations to the Cartagena Declaration on Refugees. Although not formally binding, the Cartagena Declaration on Refugees has become the basis of refugee policy in the region and has been incorporated into the national legislation of a number of states.

3. Inter-American Convention to Prevent and Punish Torture (1985)[4]

This Convention in consonance with the UDHR was adopted in 1985 and entered into force on February 28, 1987. It defines tortuous acts and renders them illegal. Member states agree to adopt national legislation following the guidelines set forth by this treaty, making any form of torture illegal under any circumstance.

Additionally, parties to the Convention agree to include torture under their list of extraditable crimes.

4. Protocol of San Salvador: Additional Protocol to the American Convention on Human Rights in the Area of Economic, Social and Cultural Rights (1988)[5]

This Additional Protocol was adopted in 1988 and entered into force on November 16, 1999. It focuses on the state's obligation to promote social, economic, and cultural human rights, such as those related to labour laws, health issues, education rights, economic rights, rights relating to the family, and rights of children, the elderly, and the handicapped. It demonstrates that states may fulfill these obligations through enacting legislation, enforcing measures of protection, and refrain from discrimination.

5. Protocol to the American Convention on Human Rights to Abolish the Death Penalty (1990)[6]

This Protocol was adopted on June 8, 1990. Any nation that is a party to the American Convention on Human Rights may sign this Protocol. Those states that sign the Protocol agree to eliminate the death penalty, although they may declare, upon signing, the intent to retain the death penalty in wartime for serious military crimes, in keeping with international law.

6. Inter-American Convention on the Forced Disappearance of Persons (1994)[7]

This Convention was adopted in 1994 and entered into force on March 28, 1996. State parties to this Convention have agreed to ban forced disappearances and to punish those who attempt to commit this crime. It specifies that one cannot use the excuses of "following orders" or "military duty" as a rationale for avoiding punishment for this crime, nor can any exceptional circumstances, such as war time, justify or legalize this act.

7. Inter-American Convention on the Prevention, Punishment and Eradication of Violence Against Women (1994)[8]

This Convention was adopted in 1994 and entered into force on

March 5, 1995. It defines violence against women as being gender based and having a negative affect on a woman's physical, sexual, or psychological well-being. It lists rights of women, including freedom from violence in both the public and private sphere, as well as freedom from discrimination. State parties are under obligation for preventing violence from occurring, for enacting appropriate relevant legislation prohibiting such violence, for providing women a just legal recourse in the case of violence, and to promote social awareness and cultural acceptance of these rights of women. Signature states must also include a report on the treatment of women within the state in its annual report to the Inter-American Commission of Women.

8. Inter-American Convention on the Elimination of All Forms of Discrimination Against Persons With Disabilities (1999)[9]

This Convention was adopted on June 7, 1999 (yet to enter into force). It defines the term "disability" as well as the phrase "discrimination against persons with disabilities". It is designed to allow disabled persons to fully integrate within society without being unjustly excluded on the basis of their disability. It calls for states to further justice for the disabled through legislation, social initiatives, education for the disabled and for others regarding acceptance of those with disabilities, and making buildings, methods of communication, recreation, offices, and homes available to be accessed by the disabled.

3.1 African Human Rights System

The Charter of the Organization of African Unity (OAU) was the first regional instrument that dealt with the protection of human rights in the continent. However, it contained very little references to the concepts of human rights since it was pre-occupied with more pressing issue such as unity, non-interference in internal affairs and liberation. However, under domestic and international pressure, African leaders adopted in 1986 the African Charter on Human and People Rights which is the first major instrument aimed at protecting human and peoples' rights in Africa. It established the African Commission on Human and Peoples' Rights with the responsibility to promote human and peoples' rights and ensure their protection in Africa. However, the lack of a judicial enforcement mechanism forced the African Union members to adopt on the 9th June 1998 a Protocol to the ACHPR establishing an African Court on Human and Peoples' Rights.

The African charter recognizes a number of civil and political rights (Article 1 to Article 24) as of protection against discrimination (Article 2) equality before law and equal protection of law (Article 3), right to life (Article 4), right to protection against slavery and other forms of degradable treatment (Article 5), right to liberty (Article 6). The Charter not only guarantees rights but also sets forth certain obligations to be performed by individuals towards his family and society, the State and other legally recognised communities and the international community. The rights and freedoms of each individual shall be exercised with due regard to the rights of others, collective security, morality and common interest. (Article 27)

An African Commission on Human and Peoples' Rights has been established within the Organisation of African Unity to promote human and peoples' rights and ensure their protection in Africa. The functions of the Commission shall be:

1. To promote human and peoples' rights and in particular:
   (a) to collect documents, undertake studies and researches on African problems in the field of human and peoples' rights, organise seminars, symposia and conferences, disseminate information, encourage national and local institutions concerned with human and peoples' rights.
   (b) to formulate and lay down, principles and rules aimed at solving legal problems relating to human and peoples' rights and fundamental freedoms upon which African Governments may base their legislation.
   (c) cooperate with other African and international institutions concerned with the promotion and protection of human and peoples' rights.

2. Ensure the protection of human and peoples' rights under conditions laid down by the present Charter.
3. Perform any other tasks which may be entrusted to it by the Assembly of Heads of State and Government.

The African Court on Human and Peoples' Rights complements the protective directive of the African Commission on Human and Peoples' Rights. The Court has the competence to take final and binding decisions on human rights violations. The competence of the African Court on Human and Peoples' Rights (Court) is based on its jurisdiction and the law that it will apply when exercising this jurisdiction. The Court has jurisdiction over all cases and disputes submitted to it regarding the interpretation and application of the African Charter on Human and Peoples' Rights (Charter), the Protocol to the Charter on the Establishment of the African Court on Human and Peoples' Rights (Court's Protocol) and any other relevant human rights instrument ratified by States that are party to a case.

The Court may, at the request of a Member State of the African Union (AU), any of the organs of the AU, provide an opinion on any legal matter relating to the Charter or any other relevant human rights instruments, provided that the subject matter of the opinion is not related to a matter being examined by the African Commission on Human and Peoples' Rights (African Commission).

The Court can also deal with all cases and disputes submitted to it concerning interpretation and application of the Charter, the Court's Protocol and any other relevant human rights instrument ratified by the States concerned.

3.4 Asian Human Rights System

Despite serious efforts, the Asian region has not been able to come out with a single Asian human rights protection system. The Association of South-East Asian Nations (ASEAN), a group of ten nation-states; namely Brunei Darussalam, Cambodia, Indonesia, Laos, Malaysia, Myanmar, Philippines, Singapore, Thailand and

Vietnam, have attempted to institute mechanisms for protection of rights and freedoms of the people of the region.

ASEAN has been making important progress in recent years towards the establishment of a regional human rights system for South-East Asia. Following the UN World Conference on Human Rights in June 1993, the ASEAN Ministerial Meeting held in Singapore in July 1993 declared that "in support of the Vienna Declaration and Programme of Action...ASEAN should also consider the establishment of an appropriate regional mechanism on human rights."[10] Following this a charter of human rights was signed by the leaders of all member states at the 13th ASEAN Summit on 20th November, 2007 and entered into force on 15, December, 2008 following ratification by all 10 member states. The Charter aims to give ASEAN a legal personality and to establish more clearly its institutional framework and rules of procedure.

The ASEAN Intergovernmental Commission on Human Rights (AICHR), were endorsed by ASEAN's Foreign Ministers on 20th July, 2009 during the 42nd ASEAN Ministerial Meeting in Thailand. ASEAN's leaders formally established the ASEAN Intergovernmental Commission on Human Rights (AICHR) on 23rd October, 2009, during the 15th ASEAN Summit. In addition to the establishment of the AICHR, other developments have been taking place regarding the establishment of human rights mechanisms and instruments for specific groups of people. On 7th April 2010, the ASEAN Commission for the Promotion and Protection of the Rights of Women and Children (ACWC) was inaugurated in Hanoi, Vietnam.

Another important regional grouping, South Asian Association for Regional Cooperation (SAARC), since its formation in 1985 have tried to address issues of socio-economic upliftment of the people of the member countries but have not laid much emphasis on instituting mechanisms for protection of the rights of the people. Again, human rights violations are serious in almost all the countries of the region. However, amidst international pressures, the SAARC Convention on Regional Arrangements for the Promotion of Child Welfare in South Asia and SAARC Convention on Prevention and Combating Trafficking in Women and Children for Prostitution were adopted in 2002. In the area of health, the SAARC Regional Strategy on HIV and AIDS (2006-2010) is available and projects are being implemented by the SAARC in collaboration with the UNAIDS. However, these piecemeal efforts are by no means enough to offer a life of dignity and security to the inhabitants of this multicultural region.

Regional institutions, over the years, are trying to create a safe human rights environment for the people of the region. To reinforce the necessity of creating more regional initiatives, Article 37 of the Vienna Declaration and Plan of Action states that "regional arrangements play a fundamental role in promoting and protecting human rights. They should reinforce universal human rights standards, as contained in international human rights instruments, and their protection". The World Conference on Human Rights endorses efforts under way to strengthen these arrangements and to increase their effectiveness, while at the same time stressing the importance of cooperation with the United Nations human rights activities. The World Conference on Human Rights reiterates the need to consider the "possibility of establishing regional and sub-regional arrangements for the promotion and protection of human rights where they do not already exist". Establishment of regional human rights mechanisms settles regional disputes without escalating matters to the UN. Again, because of the peculiarities of each region, one size fits all solution to potential human rights violations may not offer a long term solution. Hence, the need of the time is to encourage more and more regional instruments for efficient and effective promotion of human rights.

Notes

1. The First Protocol: The right to the peaceful enjoyment of possessions (Article 1); the right to education (Article 2); the right to free elections (Article 3).
   The Fourth Protocol:The right not to be imprisoned for debt (Article 1); the right to freedom of movement (Article 2); the right not to be

expelled from the territory of one's nation state (Article 3); the right of aliens (foreigners) not to suffer collective expulsion (Article 4).

The Seventh Protocol: The right of an alien not to be arbitrarily expelled (Article 1); the right to an appeal in criminal cases (Article 2); the right to compensation for wrongful conviction of a crime (Article 3); the right not to be tried or punished twice (Article 4); the right of spouses to equality (Article 5).

The Thirteenth Protocol (replacing the Sixth Protocol):The right not to suffer the death penalty even in time of war (Article 1).

Discrimination (Article 14 and the Twelfth Protocol): Article 14 of the original Convention provides the right not to suffer discrimination but it is confined to discrimination in the way the other rights in the Convention and Protocols are secured;

Article 1 of the Twelfth Protocol creates a general right not to suffer discrimination which is not restricted to the context of a Convention right.

2 http://www1.umn.edu/humanrts/oasinstr/zoas3con.htm
3 http://www.hrea.org/erc/Library/display.php?docid=469&categoryid=28&_type-32group=human rights treaties and other instruments
4 http://www1.umn.edu/humanrts/oasinstr/zoas9tor.htm
5 http://www1.umn.edu/humanrts/oasinstr/zoas10pe.htm
6 http://www1.umn.edu/humanrts/oasinstr/zoas8pdp.htm
7 http://www1.umn.edu/humanrts/oasinstree/forceddisapp.html
8 http://www1.umn.edu/humanrts/oasinstree/brazil1994.html
9 http://www1.umn.edu/humanrts/oasinstree/disabilitytreaty.html
10 http://www.aseanhrmech.org/downloads/1993_Joint_Communique.pdf

4

Promotion of Human Rights: National Institutions

Over the past few decades and especially after the era of liberalized reforms in India the issues of human rights have assumed substantial importance with groups, organizations, institutions and even the state has taken a renewed interest in protection and promotion of human rights. Nonetheless, the trajectory of the discourse has to be understood and analysed in a historical context.

4.1 Human Rights Movement in India

The genesis of the human rights movement in India can be traced back to the socio-religious reform movements started by social reformers as of Raja Rammohun Roy, Ishwar Chandra Vidyasagar and others. The question of women's emancipation by campaigning for abolition of *sati*, widow remarriage, women's education—all raised pertinent human rights concerns. In fact, the first human rights organization was the Indian Reform Association founded by Keshab Chandra Sen as early as 1870, even before the formation of the Indian National Congress. The association started a movement for creating a casteless society, quite a radical movement in terms of the socio-religious conditions of caste ridden India.

Mention may be made of the Brahmo movement (1878) which carried out a consistent struggle for removal of *Purdah* system, introduction of widow remarriage, abolition of polygamy and early marriage and provision for higher education. The non-Brahman movement launched by Jotiba Phule to uplift the downtrodden was, undoubtedly, a human rights movement which later on was spearheaded by Dr. B.R. Ambedkar resulting in the abolition of Untouchability and guaranteeing protection, rights and resources to the *dalits* through different constitutional and legislative provisions. Narayan Guru, another spiritual leader of Kerala launched a struggle for self-respect for the lower castes in south India and inculcated a spirit of democratic temperament among the outcastes and bringing them into the fold of the anti-colonial struggle.

After the formation of the Indian National Congress (INC), the anti-colonial movement specifically took the shape of a human rights movement by demanding specific rights from the British government. In fact, the struggle against the Rowlatt Act which sought to lock up anybody for any length of time without trial is one of the finest examples of struggles for protection of civil liberties taking the shape of a non-cooperation movement. "As a part of the freedom movement, the nationalist leadership strived to give a sense of direction to the campaign for civil liberties".[1]

The demand for human rights was popularized by INC through a number of resolutions adopted in the different sessions of the Congress between1917-1919. The first human rights group in the country was formed by Jawaharlal Nehru—the Civil Liberties Union to assist the nationalists in providing legal aid.

In all these movements for reform, although the phrase human rights was not mentioned, yet all these were an attempt towards granting people a life with dignity, the philosophy behind all human rights movement around the world. Another point deserves mention is the fact that all the issues of contemporary social movements have their roots in our past.

The Constitution of India influenced by the Universal Declaration of Human Rights incorporated a series of civil and political rights in Part III of the Constitution to display the image of a rights friendly state but simultaneously too kept powers to take away rights in the name of national or state emergency. While the INC revolted against the Rowlatt Bills and initiated the non-cooperation movement in protest, after independence the same

Congress inserted Article 22 (Preventive Detention), an attempt to detain people on the apprehension that if they are left free they might pose a danger to the integrity of the country.

The decade just after independence was a period of giving a chance to the new state to meet the aspirations of the people. However, a new resurgence of human rights movement started during the nineteen month National Emergency imposed by Mrs Indira Gandhi between 1975-1977. The period witnessed the widest possible violation of human rights at the hands of a democratic government and marginalization of the already marginalized segment of the society. But the question is why a civil rights movement started when the Constitution appeared to fulfill the basic rights of the Indians.

The development-growth model introduced by the Nehruvian state failed to achieve the desired results. The Green revolution, no doubt, increased production but also at the same time widened disparities between classes and across regions.[2] The period also witnessed economic deterioration in the guise of devaluation of the Rupee (1966), inflation, severe drought and an overall fall in standard of living. Nehru's socialism was waning away. The JP movement and the Naxalite movement steered human rights issues but due to governmental repression, the movements gradually lost ground.

The emergency came as a bitter tragedy to the liberal intellectuals and middle class. Massive repression was let loose—arbitrary detention, torture, killing deaths—characterized the period. The people were deprived of their basic rights. Rule of law was completely eroded and the entire institutional mechanism of the state functioned on an authoritarian model. Under such conditions, societal response against the repressive measures of the government provided the stimulus for civil liberties movement in the country. Herein one thing needs to be mentioned, the civil liberties movement was not for securing new rights but for making available the rights already there in the Constitution.

Human rights have been taking shape in the country after the emergency and have raised issues pertaining to the economically marginalized and socially excluded peoples. With the opening up of state boundaries to global multinational forces, the different disparate movements have formed alliances, both national and international to counter the dominance of global economic and political power. Globalization has intensified the already existing economic and social inequalities, deepening regional, sub-regional movements.

The human rights movements since the post-cold war period has moved beyond the demand for civil liberties. As D. L. Sheth observes, "the politics of micro-movements, therefore, lies, not merely in fighting particular infringements of legal rights of citizens, but in creating and expanding new political and civic spaces for them by converting the survival and development needs of the poor and the deprived into struggles for their economic, political and cultural rights and these not only of individuals qua individuals but of groups and communities surviving on the margins of the civil society".[3]

Again, all the movements irrespective of issues and participants converge on the same point of equity and justice. It is interesting to note that the major ecological, women and civil society movements going on in the country raise the demand for a life with human dignity and the right to human security.

The State has also taken a pro-active role in protecting rights by creating institutions for safeguarding the rights of the common Indians. In consonance with the International Covenant on Civil and Political Rights, the Protection of Human Rights Act was enacted in 1993 which created the National Human Rights Commission and State Human Rights Commissions to respond to violations of rights.

National Human Rights Commission

The National Human Rights Commission (NHRC) was constituted under the Protection of Human Rights Act of 1993. One of the objectives of the Act was the establishment of NHRC for better protection and promotion of human rights as enshrined in the UDHR.

(I) Composition of National Human Rights Commission

The Commission shall consist of :

(1) a Chairperson who has been a Chief Justice of the Supreme Court;
(2) one Member who is or has been, a Judge of the Supreme Court;
(3) one Member who is, or has been, the Chief Justice of a High Court;
(4) two Members to be appointed from amongst persons having knowledge of, or practical experience in, matters relating to human rights.
In addition to this there will be three ex-officio member of the Commission:
(6) The Chairperson of the National Commission for Minorities.
(7) The Chairperson of the National Commission for the Scheduled Castes and Scheduled Tribes, and
(8) The Chairperson of the National Commission for Women

Besides these nominated members there is a Secretary-General who is the Chief Executive Officer of the Commission and exercises such powers and discharges such functions of the Commission as may be delegated to him.

(II) Appointment of Chairperson and other Members of NHRC

The Chairperson and other Members of the Commission are appointed by the President of India after obtaining the recommendations of a Committee consisting of:

(a) The Prime Minister
(b) Speaker of the Lok Sabha;
(c) Minister in-charge of the Ministry of Home Affairs in the Government of India;
(d) Leader of the Opposition in the House of the People;

(e) Leader of the Opposition in the Council of States;
(f) Deputy Chairman of the Rajya Sabha.

(III) Removal of a Member of the Commission

The Chairperson or any other Member of the Commission shall only be removed from his office by order of the President on the ground of proved misbehaviour or incapacity, after the Supreme Court, on reference being made to it by the President, has, on inquiry held in accordance with the procedure prescribed in that behalf by the Supreme Court, reported that the Chairperson or such other Member, as the case may be, ought on any such ground to be removed. The President may remove the Chairperson or any other Member if he:

(a) is adjudged an insolvent; or
(b) engages during his term of office in any paid employment outside the duties of his office: or
(c) is unfit to continue in office by reason of infirmity of mind or body; or
(d) is of unsound mind and stands so declared by a competent court; or
(e) is convicted and sentenced to imprisonment for an offence which in the opinion of the President involves moral turpitude.

(IV) Term of office of Members

According to Section 6 of the Protection of Human Rights Act, 1993, Chairperson shall hold office for a term of five years from the date on which he enters upon his office or until he attains the age of seventy years, whichever is earlier. A Member shall hold office for a term of five years from the date on which he enters upon his office and shall be eligible for re-appointment for another term of five years, provided that no Member shall hold office after he has attained the age of seventy years.

(V) Functions of the Commission

The Commission performs following functions:

(a) inquires, *suomotu* or on a petition presented to it by a victim or any person on his behalf, on the violation of human rights or abetment thereof and negligence by a public servant in the prevention of such violation;

(b) intervenes in any proceeding involving any allegation of violation of human rights pending before a court with the approval of such court;

(c) visits, under intimation to the State Government, any jail or any other institution under the control of the State Government, where persons are detained or lodged for purposes of treatment, reformation or protection to study the living conditions of the inmates and make recommendations thereon;

(d) reviews the safeguards provided by or under the Constitution or any law for the time being in force for the protection of human rights and recommend measures for their effective implementation;

(e) reviews the factors, including acts of terrorism that inhibit the enjoyment of human rights and recommend appropriate remedial measures;

(f) studies treaties and other international instruments on human rights and make recommendations for their effective implementation;

(g) undertakes and promotes research in the field of human rights;

(h) spreads human rights literacy among various sections of society and promotes awareness of the safeguards available for the protection of these rights through publications, media, seminars and other available means;

(i) encourages the efforts of non-governmental organizations and institutions working in the field of human rights;

(j) such other functions as it may consider necessary for the protection of human rights.

(VI) Matters not subject to jurisdiction of the Commission

(1) The Commission shall not inquire into any matter which is pending before a State Commission or any other Commission duly constituted under any law for the time being in force.
(2) The Commission or the State Commission shall not inquire into any matter after the expiry of one year from the date on which the act constituting violation of human rights is alleged to have been committed.

When the Commission was established, there was a lot of cynicism. To some it was going to be a 'toothless tiger', while others found it another superfluous mechanism promising too much but would deliver little. Despite such pessimistic observations the Commission has some achievements to its credit. The number of cases filed in the NHRC has significantly increased to 17298 as of May, 2012 which shows people's faith in the machinery. It has succeeded in persuading the Central Government to sign the United Nations Convention against Torture and Other Forms of Cruel, Inhuman and Degrading Punishment or Treatment. It has vehemently criticized the problem of custodial deaths and taken steps to see that these are not suppressed by the state agencies, introduced reforms in prisons. It has also helped in creating awareness on human rights by designing specialised training modules for police forces, students, teachers and for the general citizenry. Despite all these efforts the Commission has not been able to completely minimize cases of violations primarily due to the fact that it cannot enforce its decisions. It can merely offer its recommendations to the government and it is up to the Government to accept or reject.

State Human Rights Commission

The Protection of Human Rights Act, 1993 also provides for establishment of State Human Rights Commission (SHRC) in respective states to monitor protection of human rights. The SHRC consist of:

(1) a Chairperson who has been a Chief Justice of the High Court;
(2) one Member who is or has been, a Judge of a High Court;
(3) one Member who is, or has been, a District Judge in that State;
(4) two Members to be appointed from amongst persons having knowledge of, or practical experience in, matters relating to human rights.

The Chairperson and other members shall be appointed by the Governor on the basis of the recommendation of a Committee constituting of the Chief Minister, Speaker of the Legislative Assembly, Minister-in-charge of the Department of Home in that State and leader of Opposition in the Legislative Assembly.

The powers and functions of the Commission are almost the same within the State as that of the NHRC.

National Commission for Women

The National Commission for Women was established in 1992 under the National Commission for Women Act, 1990. The Commission shall consist of:

1. A Chairperson, committed to the cause of women, to be nominated by the Central Government;
2. Five members to be nominated by the Central Government from amongst persons who have expertise in law, trade unionism, women's voluntary organizations, administration, health, education, social welfare;
3. A Member-Secretary to be nominated by the Central Government from amongst experts in field of management, organizational structure or sociological movement.

The functions of the Commission

To examine and investigate all matters relating to the safeguards provided for women in the Indian Constitution and the laws.

To provide reports to the Central Government on the working of the safeguards.

To make recommendations for effective implementation of the safeguards and for improving the conditions of women.

To review existing laws and suggest remedial legislative measures to overcome the lacunae in them.

Look into complaints and take *suo motu* action on matters relating to deprivation of women's rights, failure to implement laws aimed at gender equality.

Undertake promotional and educational research for ensuring due representation of women in all spheres.

Inspect women's remand home, place of custody and take necessary action.

Make periodic reports to the Government on any matter pertaining to women.

The National Commission for Minorities

The National Commission for Minorities created under the National Commission of Minorities Act, 1992. The Commission shall consist of a Chairperson, [a Vice Chairperson and five] Members to be nominated by the Central Government from amongst persons of eminence, ability and integrity; Provided that five Members including the Chairperson shall be from amongst the Minority communities.

The Commission shall perform all or any of the following functions, namely:

(a) evaluate the progress of the development of Minorities under the Union and States.
(b) monitor the working of the safeguards provided in the Constitution and in laws enacted by Parliament and the State Legislatures.
(c) make recommendations for the effective implementation of safeguards for the protection of the interests of Minorities by the Central Government or the State Governments.

(d) look into specific complaints regarding deprivation of rights and safeguards of the Minorities and take up such matters with the appropriate authorities.
(e) cause studies to be undertaken into problems arising out of any discrimination against Minorities and recommend measures for their removal.
(f) conduct studies, research and analysis on the issues relating to socio-economic and educational development of Minorities.
(g) suggest appropriate measures in respect of any Minority to be undertaken by the Central Government or the State Governments.
(h) make periodical or special reports to the Central Government on any matter pertaining to Minorities and in particular the difficulties confronted by them.
(i) any other matter which may be referred to it by the Central Government.

The National Commission for Scheduled Castes

The National Commission for Scheduled Castes was created in 2004. It shall be the duty of the Commission –

(a) to investigate and monitor all matters relating to the safeguards provided for the Scheduled Castes under this Constitution or under any other law for the time being in force or under any order of the Government and to evaluate the working of such safeguards;
(b) to inquire into specific complaints with respect to the deprivation of rights and safeguards of the Scheduled Castes;
(c) to participate and advise on the planning process of socio-economic development of the Scheduled Castes and to evaluate the progress of their development under the Union and any State;
(d) to present to the President, annually and at such other times as the Commission may deem fit, reports upon the working of those safeguards;

(e) to make in such reports recommendations as to the measures that should be taken by the Union or any State for the effective implementation of those safeguards and other measures for the protection, welfare and socio-economic development of the Scheduled Castes; and

(f) to discharge such other functions in relation to the protection, welfare and development and advancement of the Scheduled Castes as the President may, subject to the provisions of any law made by Parliament, by rule specify.

(g) to make in such reports recommendations as to the measures that should be taken by the Union or any State for the effective implementation of those safeguards and other measures for the protection, welfare and socio-economic development of the Scheduled Castes; and

(h) to discharge such other functions in relation to the protection, welfare and development and advancement of the Scheduled Castes as the President may, subject to the provisions of any law made by Parliament, by rule specify.

The National Commission for Scheduled Tribes

The National Commission for Scheduled Tribes (NCST) was established by amending Article 338 and inserting a new Article 338A in the Constitution through the Constitution (89th Amendment) Act, 2003. By this amendment, the erstwhile National Commission for Scheduled Castes and Scheduled Tribes was replaced by two separate Commissions namely—

(i) the National Commission for Scheduled Castes (NCSC), and

(ii) the National Commission for Scheduled Tribes (NCST).

The Functions of the NCST are:

1. To investigate and Monitor matters relating to Safeguards provided for STs under the Constitution or under other laws;

2. To inquire into specific complaints relating to Rights and Safeguards of STs;
3. To participate and advise in the Planning Process relating to Socio-economic development of STs, and to evaluate the progress of their development under the Union and any State;
4. To submit report to the President annually and at such other times as the Commission may deem fit, upon/working of Safeguards, Measures required for effective implementation of Programmers/Schemes relating to Welfare and Socio-economic development of STs;
5. The Commission would also discharge the following other functions in relation to the protection, welfare and development and advancement of the Scheduled Tribes, namely—
   (i) Measures that need to be taken over conferring ownership rights in respect of minor forest produce to the Scheduled Tribes living in forest areas.
   (ii) Measures to be taken to safeguard rights to the Tribal Communities over mineral resources, water resources etc. as per law.
   (iii) Measures to be taken for the development of tribals and to work for move viable livelihood strategies.
   (iv) Measures to be taken to improve the efficacy of relief and rehabilitation measures for tribal groups displaced by development projects.
   (v) Measures to be taken to prevent alienation of tribal people from land and to effectively rehabilitate such people in whose case alienation has already taken place.
   (vi) Measures to be taken to elicit maximum cooperation and involvement of Tribal Communities for protecting forests and undertaking social afforestation.
   (vii) Measures to be taken to ensure full implementation of the Provisions of Panchayats (Extension to the Scheduled Areas) Act, 1996 (40 of 1996).

With the establishment of NHRC and other sister agencies, India has made significant progress in protecting the rights of her people. Yet everything is not done. Protection of rights is not a one time affair but a work in progress. Powerful elements, interest groups, wealthy segments, corrupt elements still exploit the rights of others. Besides, large chunks of the population are still unaware of their rights, let alone know of the existence of mechanisms to protect their rights. Needless to say, only establishment of mechanisms will not create a positive environment for rights. What is perhaps most important is truly empowering these mechanisms as well as creating full awareness of human rights through education, training and instilling confidence in the minds of people, especially the marginalized.

Notes

1. G. Haragopal & K. Balagopal, "Civil Liberties Movement and the State in India" in Manoranjan Mohanty, Partha Nath Mukherji & Olle Tornquist (ed.), *People's Rights: Social Movements and the State in the Third World*, Sage Publications, New Delhi, 1998, p. 355.
2. *Ibid.*
3. D. L. Sheth, *Globalization and New Politics of Micro-Movements*, www.democracy-asia.org/resources on democracy/globalization%20&%20_the%20/new%20politics%20of%20micro-movements.

Section II
Issues in Human Rights

5

The Vulnerables: The Children and the Aged

"The children of the world are innocent, vulnerable and dependent. They are also curious, active and full of hope. Their time should be one of joy and peace, of playing, learning and growing. Their future should be shaped in harmony and cooperation. Their lives should mature, as they broaden their perspectives and gain new experience". This is the message which emanate from the World Declaration on the Survival Protection and Development of Children. The plight of the children is miserable and everyday they are subjected to countless dangers raising questions regarding their survival and the enjoyment of human rights.

Though regarded as citizens of tomorrow, yet children are the most vulnerable of all throughout the world. Innocence, lack of awareness, improper care and guidance make them easy prey to deprivation and abuse. Crimes against children as of child labour, child abuse, trafficking are issues of serious concern both nationally and internationally. Moreover, crimes such as female infanticide, foeticide, child marriage, abandoning the baby girl intentionally are serious crimes threatening the survival of the female child. In fact this is one of the major reasons behind the imbalance in the sex ratio in the country. Children are often beaten, sexually exploited; again sold to unscrupulous traders to be turned into beggars, domestic servants and employed in hazardous jobs as of stone quarrying, beedi making, fireworks, carpet weaving etc. It seems imperative to accept the fact that child problems should not be studied in isolation; it is directly related to parents, family upbringing and societal systems.

International Conventions

The Geneva Declaration of the Rights of the Child (1924) affirms that it is the duty of men and women of all nations to ensure that the child must be given the means requisite for its normal development, both materially and spiritually and must be protected from all forms of exploitation.

Furthermore, the UDHR affirms the right to a dignified life for all including children and guarantees certain civil, social, economic and cultural rights to them.

Article 3: Everyone has the right to life, liberty and security of person.

Article 4: No one shall be held in slavery or servitude: slavery and the slave trade shall be prohibited in all their forms.

Article 15: Everyone has the right to a nationality. No one shall be arbitrarily deprived of his nationality nor denied the right to change his nationality.

Article 25: Everyone has a right to a standard of living adequate for the health and well-being of himself and of his family, including food, clothing, housing and medical care and necessary social service and the right to security in the event of unemployment, sickness, disability, widowhood, old age or lack of livelihood in circumstances beyond his control.

Motherhood and childhood are entitled to special care and assistance. All children, whether born in or out of wedlock shall enjoy the same social protection.

Article 26: Everyone has the right to education. Education shall be free at least in the elementary and fundamental stages. Elementary education shall be compulsory. Technical and professional education shall be made generally available and higher education shall be equally accessible to all on the basis of merit.

Education shall be directed to the full development of the human personality and to the strengthening of respect for human rights and fundamental freedoms. It shall promote understanding, tolerance and friendship among all nation, racial or religious groups, and shall further the activities of the United Nations for the maintenance of peace.

Parents have a prior right to choose the kind of education that shall be given to their children.

Another milestone for protection of rights of child is the **Declaration of the Rights of the Child (1959)** which *recognises that* children, because of their physical and mental immaturity, need special safeguards and care, including appropriate legal protection, before as well as after birth. All children are entitled to some basic rights as to:

- Right to social security.
- Right to health.
- Right to adequate nutrition, housing, recreation and medical services.
- Right to education.
- Right to play, leisure and recreation.
- Protection against all forms of cruelty, neglect and exploitation.
- Physically, mentally or socially handicapped children should be given special treatment, education and care required by his particular condition.
- Society and the public authorities shall have the duty to extend particular care to children without a family and to those without adequate means of support.

The Convention provides for a cluster of rights but mentioned no mechanism for implementation of these rights. To guarantee security and a happy childhood, the **Convention on the Rights of the Child** was adopted in 1989. This is the most important international document on child rights and protection. It consists of a set of international standards for promoting and protecting rights of children. State Parties are under an obligation to ensure that suitable environment is created for healthy growth and development of children. Children are neither the property of their parents nor are they helpless objects of charity. They are human beings and are the subject of their own rights. By recognizing children's rights in this way, the Convention firmly sets the focus on the whole child. The essential rights of children can be broadly segmented into four categories:

(i) **The Right to Survival**: It includes right to a life, the highest attainable standard of health, nutrition and adequate standard of living. It also includes the right to name and nationality.
(ii) **The Right to Protection:** It includes freedom from all forms of exploitation, abuses, inhuman or degrading treatment and negligence including the right to special protection in situation of emergency and armed conflicts.
(iii) **The Right to Development**: It includes right to education, social security, right to leisure, recreation and cultural activities.
(iv) **The Right to Participation:** It includes freedom of expression, access to appropriate information, freedom of thought, conscience and religion.

The **Committee on the Rights of the Child** has been established to monitor implementation of the standards prescribed in the Convention. State Parties have to submit periodic reports regarding the progress made in the implementation of the safeguards outlined in the Declaration.

The World Declaration on the Survival, Protection, and Development of Children (1990) is committed towards the well-being of children which requires political action at the highest level. It focuses on enhancement of children's health and nutrition and for according care and support to disabled children, as well as to other children in very difficult circumstances. Provision of basic education and literacy for all is among the most important contributions that can be made to the development of the world's children. It also assigns strengthening of the role of women in general and ensuring their equal rights for the benefit of the world's children. Safe motherhood must be promoted in all possible ways.

Emphasis must be placed on responsible planning of family size and on child spacing. The family, as a fundamental group and natural environment for the growth and well-being of children, should be given all necessary protection and assistance. All children must be given the chance to find their identity and realize their worth in a safe and supportive environment, through families and other care-givers committed to their welfare. They must be prepared for responsible life in a free society. They should, from their early years, be encouraged to participate in the cultural life of their societies.

The Summit emphasized the need for a concerted Plan of Action, as a framework for more specific national and international undertakings. In 2002, the General Assembly in a resolution adopted a document entitled 'A world fit for children' wherein State Parties reaffirmed their obligation to take action to promote and protect the rights of each child – every human being below the age of 18 years, including adolescents. A number of principles and objectives were adopted which are as follows:

- Put children first.
- Eradicate poverty: invest in children.
- Leave no child behind.
- Care for every child.
- Educate every child.
- Protect children from harm and exploitation.
- Protect children from war.
- Combat HIV/AIDS.
- Listen to children and ensure their participation.
- Protect the Earth for children.

In line with these principles and objectives, a Plan of Action was also formulated to build a world where children would be loved and lead a discrimination-free life.

Indian Constituion and Children

The framers of the Constitution were aware of the plight of children and realized their need for special care and protection. Hence a number of provisions were incorporated much before the Conventions of the Rights of Child was adopted in 1959.

Article 15(3) Special provisions may be made by State for women and children.

Article 21 (A) Right to free and compulsory education for children up to the age of 14 years.

Article 23(1) Prohibition of human trafficking, forced labour, beggary etc.

Article 24 Prohibits employment of children below 14 years

Article 39 The State should direct its policy towards ensuring that the health and strength of workers and the tender age of children are not abused.

Directive Principles in Constitution of India also provide protection for the children such as, Article 39 (e), Article 39 (f), Article 41, Article 42, Article 45, and Article 47.

Article 51 A clause (k) and (j): The parent or the guardian to provide opportunities for education to his child or as case may be ward between the age of 6-14 years.

National Laws and Commissions

While all children have equal rights, their situations are not uniform. At the same time, childhood and the range of children's needs and rights are one whole, and must be addressed holistically. A life-cycle approach must be maintained. Keeping this in mind, there are several national laws and policies that address the different age-groups and categories of children.

1956	Immoral Traffic (Prevention) Act, Amended in 1986.
1960	Orphanages and other Charitable Homes (Supervision and Control) Act.
1974	National Policy for Children.
1986	Child Labour (Prohibition and Regulation) Act.
2000	Juvenile Justice (Care and Protection of Children) Act.
2006	Protection of Child Marriage Act.
2006	Juvenile Justice (Care and Protection of Children) Amendment Act.
2009	The Right of Children to Free and Compulsory Education Act.

In 1974, the Government of India adopted a National Policy for Children, declaring the nation's children as 'supremely important assets'. This policy lays down recommendations for a comprehensive health programme, supplementary nutrition for mothers and children, nutrition education for mothers, free and compulsory education for all children up to the age of 14, non-formal pre-school education, promotion of physical education and recreational activities, special consideration for the children of weaker sections of the population like the Scheduled Castes and the Scheduled Tribes, prevention of exploitation of children and special facilities for children with handicaps.

The policy provided for a National Children's Board to act as a forum to plan, review and coordinate the various services directed toward children. The Board was first set up in 1974.

The Department of Women and Child Development was set up in the Ministry of Human Resource Development in 1985. The Department, besides ICDS, implements several other programmes, undertakes advocacy and inter-sectoral monitoring catering to the needs of women and children. In pursuance of this, the Department formulated a National Plan of Action for Children in 1992. The Government of India ratified the Convention on the Rights of the Child on 12th November, 1992. By ratifying the Convention on the Rights of the Child, the Government is obligated "to review National and State legislation and bring it in line with provisions of the Convention".

National Commission for Protection of Child Rights, 2007[1]: The National Commission for Protection of Child Rights (NCPCR) was set up in March 2007 under the Commission for Protection of Child Rights Act, 2005, an Act of Parliament (December, 2005). The Commission's primary responsibility is to ensure that all laws, policies, programmes, and administrative mechanisms are in consonance with the Child Rights perspective as enshrined in the Constitution of India and also the UN Convention on the Rights of the Child.

The Commission envisages a rights-based perspective to be a part of all National Policies and Programmes, along with nuanced responses at the State, District and Block levels, taking care of specificities and strengths of each region. In order to touch every child, it seeks a deeper penetration to communities and households and expects that the ground experiences inform the support the field receives from all the authorities at the higher level. Thus, the Commission sees an indispensable role for the State, sound institution-building processes, respect for decentralization at the local level and larger societal concern for children and their well-being.

Despite the existence of rights, policies, laws, both national and international, children suffer from poverty, homelessness, abuse, neglect, preventable diseases, unequal access to education and justice systems that do not recognize their special needs. These are problems that occur in both industrialized and developing countries. The need of the hour is to sensitize citizens of the vulnerable position of children and carry out a comprehensive action plan to give them a safe, secure and happy childhood.

Rights of Elderly

The twenty first century may have achieved the impossible but it has not yet been able to arrest ageing. No one can defy the fact that everyone of our young generation will be old some day. Sadly, had the government promised us social security we would not have suffered from this impending devil 'old age'. However, it is only a small segment of the total population who enjoy the comforts of retired life. The 2001 census has shown that the elderly population (60+) of India accounted for 77 million and census 2011 projections indicate that elderly population has crossed the 100 million mark. The life expectancy has also gone up to 70+ years today. Better medical facilities, care and liberal family planning policies made the elderly the fastest growing section of the society in India. Simultaneously with higher life expectancy, the complexities associated with old age has also gone higher. The ensuing discussion seeks to focus on the complexities of elderly persons due to violation of their rights and the international and national efforts in giving them a peaceful life.

With fast industrialization and consumerism, rapid changes are taking place at the societal and domestic level. The disintegration of the joint family system has deprived the elder members of their prestige and power and subjected them to a life of isolation. Today senior citizens are mere caretakers of nuclear families devoid of any authority. Added to this is the fact that very few avenues are left open to them after formal retirement. Because of age they also lack the initiative and courage to fight for their rights primarily because the violators are their very own family members. Furthermore, in a country like India, a substantial portion of old people are illiterate and unaware of their rights. Social marginalization, loneliness, isolation and even negligence in old age lead violation of Human Rights of Older Persons.[2]

Problems of Elderly and Human Rights Violations

When the Universal Declaration of Human Rights was drafted, it unequivocally declared protection and promotion of rights for **all**. Article 1 of the UDHR promises everyone a life of freedom and dignity. Article 25 of Universal Declaration of Human Rights provides that everyone has the right to a standard of living adequate for the health and well-being of himself and of his family, including food, clothing, housing and medical care and necessary social services, and the right to security in the event of unemployment, sickness, disability, widowhood, old age or other lack of livelihood in circumstances beyond his control. Many international and national efforts have been initiated for different sections of the people—children, women, refugees, stateless persons, indigenous peoples but for quite a few decades the UN was silent and quite complacent about the needs of the elderly who were and are still the silent sufferers. With a few exceptions they suffer from financial insecurity primarily due to lack of governmental pension policies, or unavailability of other means of livelihood, Emotional/psychological insecurity because of increased migration within families in search of better opportunities; diseases/old age related ailments due to costly medical facilities and in remote areas often basic medical facilities are unavailable. Furthermore, there appears to be a huge generation gap and the younger ones are not ready to give them time to or be a partner to their parents/grandparents. Due to apathy and lack of enthusiasm very few organizations are interested in working for the aged. The aged themselves are not in a position to demand their rights and hence we do not find much of movements spearheaded by aged and for the rights of aged. With the elderly having to spend much of their post-retirement lives in the four walls of their home, even the print or the audio-visual media have not been able to reach out to these significant and potential viewers. Hardly do we find programmes made and telecast to cater to the needs of the elderly. With the media increasingly interfering into our private domain why is it silent towards our parents and grandparents' entertainment? It is high time to redress the neglect meted out to them.

International Efforts

Till the 1970s, the aged remained outside the purview of human rights conventions, treaties, declarations and were the most neglected lot. In 1982 for the first time, the World Assembly on Ageing was held in Vienna to discuss the problems faced by the aged to health and nutrition, protection of elderly consumers, housing, social welfare, family, income, security, unemployment, and education throughout the world. The outcome of the Conference was the adoption of the International Plan of Action on Ageing. The plan attempted to provide a blueprint to member countries to deal with the needs and concerns of elderly. On the basis of this Plan of Action, the General Assembly in 1991, adopted the United Nations Principles for Older Persons on independence, participation, care, self-fulfillment and dignity of the elderly.

To maintain independence, older persons should:

- Have access to adequate food, water, shelter, clothing, health through the provision of income, family, community;

- Have the opportunity to work or to have access to other in generating opportunities and be able to decide when to leave work;
- Have access to appropriate educational and training programme;
- To live in a safe environment according to personal preferences.

To enable participation

- They should participate actively in the formulation and implementation of policies for their well-being.
- Be able to form movements or associations for older persons.

To get care

- Have access to health care, and a high degree of emotional well-being and benefit from family and community protection.

For their self-fulfillment

- Older persons should be able to pursue opportunities for the full development of their potential.
- Have access to the educational, cultural, spiritual and recreational resources of society.

For their dignity

- They should be able to live in dignity and security and be free of exploitation and physical or mental abuse.
- Be treated fairly and be valued independently of their economic contribution.

The General Assembly subsequently deliberated on the way forward of these principles and 1999 was declared as the International Year of the Older Persons. In April 2002, the United

Nations revisited the rights of the elderly at the Second World Conference on Ageing in Madrid, and reviewed the recommendations adopted in the Vienna Plan. "The Conference resulted in the International Plan of Action ("the Madrid Plan"), adopted by 159 countries and calling for the promotion and protection of all human rights and fundamental freedoms, including the right to development, the need to include ageing in global agendas, and the need to combat discrimination based on age".[3] The recommendations are organized according to three priorities:

- Older Persons and Development,
- Advancing Health and Well-Being into Old Age,
- Ensuring Enabling and Supportive Environments.

The Madrid Plan includes recommendations aimed at implementation and follow-up. It entrusts the international, regional and national human rights forums for translating the policies into actions. However, the Madrid Plan fails to be a binding document to impose obligations upon signatory states. "Another example of a specialized agency relevant to the rights of the elderly (although with less legal relevance) is the World Health Organization **("WHO")**. This agency has dealt with the issue of elderly health regarding medical care and social welfare from a technical perspective of gerontology and geriatrics, as well as demography and clinical studies".[4]

National Efforts

The framers of the constitution did not give much thought for the elderly except for just one Directive Principle in Article 41 which states that the State shall, within the limits of economic capacity and development, make effective provision for securing the right to work, to education and to public assistance in cases of unemployment, old age, sickness and disablement, and in other cases of undeserved want. This is just a directive towards good governance but does not create binding obligations on the government. In the guise of welfare a number of services and schemes have been announced for the elderly but they remain mostly on paper.

In 1999, the Central Government approved the National Policy for Older Persons to empower elderly. This policy provided for the establishment of a pension fund for the unorganized sector' construction of old age homes, recreate source of re-employment for the able elderly, concessional rates for air/train journey within India, sensitive taxation policies for senior citizens, special bank rate interest. The Maintenance and Welfare of Parents and Senior Citizens Act, 2007 seeks to ensure safety, security, care and dignity of senior citizens.

The last few decades have witnessed serious loss of values among the young generation and therefore, just making of laws or policies are not sufficient. What is urgently needed is a sense of concern for the aged and restoration of our societal values and customs. Citizens need to be sensitized to the needs of them and more importantly they should be looked as treasure house of love and experience rather than a burden. The policies need to be implemented with a human touch rather than as stereotype laws. The interests of the elderly can be met by compassion, care and respect and being sensitive towards their emotional and physical well-being. Let us age gracefully and let us strive to make our senior citizens live a long happy life.

Notes

1. www.ncpcr.gov.in
2. *Human Rights of Older Persons in India: A National Study*, Agewell Research and Advocay Centre, www.agewellfoundation.org
3. As quoted in Diego Rodriguez-Pinzon and Claudia Martin, "The International Human Rights Status of Elderly Persons." *American University International Law Review 18*, No. 4 (2003): 915-1008.
4. *Ibid.*

6

Cultural Diversity and Human Rights

Managing cultural diversity, being, one of the fundamental challenges of our times, most of the states all-over the world such as India, Nigeria, Mexico, South Africa, Sri Lanka, Somalia, Iraq, Iran, Turkey, Canada, Australia, Britain and Spain are pre-occupied with handling tribulations stemming from ethno-nationalism in their individual territories. Moreover, in the post-Cold war period and in the wake of recent social transformations, cultural diversity has increasingly shaped the foundations of majority of social conflicts and political deliberations. Identity questions have assumed preponderance with ethnicities increasingly demanding recognition, resources and rights. As S.P. Huntington in his *The Clash of Civilizations and the Remaking of World Order* observes:

> "In the post-Cold war period, the most important distinctions among peoples are not ideological, political or economic. They are cultural. People define themselves in terms of ancestry, religion, language, history, values, customs and institutions. They identify with cultural groups: tribes, ethnic groups, religious communities, nations, and at the broadest level civilizations".[1]

In this era of globalization and rapid social transformation, cultural diversity lies at the heart of contemporary debates about identity and social cohesion. Globalization processes, facilitated by the rapid development of information and communication technologies, are often perceived to be eroding cultural diversity, making the preservation of diversity all the more important. In multicultural societies maintenance of unity necessitates an intercultural dialogue and harmonious interaction between individuals and groups and an accommodative policy for fostering diversity.

Such accommodation calls for an environment that safeguards fundamental freedoms and human rights, which are universal, inalienable, interconnected and interdependent. "No one may invoke cultural diversity as an excuse to infringe on human rights guaranteed by international law or limit their scope, nor should cultural diversity be taken to support segregation and harmful traditional practices which, in the name of culture, seek to sanctify differences that run counter to the universality, indivisibility and interdependence of human rights".[2]

The issue of guaranteeing cultural rights has assumed added importance after the collapse of three multicultural federations—Soviet Union, Yugoslavia, Czechoslovakia. At a time when the problems of refugees, ethno-centrism, racial discrimination, religious wars, linguistic clashes is raising new challenges to the world community how can diverse communities and groups live together. How can human rights be reconciled with the clash of cultures that has come to characterize our time? Cultural identity, today, is a prime source of group consciousness giving rise to inter- and intra-group conflicts.

Universal Human Rights and Cultural Relativism

"Culture is a historically created system of meaning and significance or, what comes to the same thing, a system of beliefs and practices in terms of which a group of human beings understand, regulate and structure their individual and collective lives".[3] Simply speaking, culture is essentially a way of life manifested both within an objective and a subjective dimension. The objective element is reflected in characteristics such as language and dialects, religious practices, or customs, traditions, symbols whilst the subjective dimension is reflected in mutually shared attitudes and feelings. Again, culture has both an individual and a collective dimension.

Culture is mostly considered to be important to human beings. In other words, culture may give individuals and communities a sense of belonging. Again cultural diversity is also an important constituent and condition of human freedom. "Unless human beings are able to step out of their culture, they remain imprisoned within it and tend to absolutize it... and they cannot step out of their culture unless they have access to others".[4] This is where human rights come into play.

Another matter impeding the development of cultural rights is the debate between the theories of universalism and cultural relativism. Universalism emphasizes that all human beings are entitled to basic human rights by virtue of being human, irrespective of any other considerations. These rights are inalienable and are indispensable for the promotion of human dignity. However, there is nothing wrong in this proposition since the Universal Declaration of Human Rights unequivocally declares: "*[All human beings are born equal in dignity and rights. They are endowed with reason and conscience and should act towards one another in a spirit of brotherhood.*"(Article 1)

Article 2 continues: "*Everyone is entitled to all the rights and freedoms set forth in this Declaration, without distinction of any kind such as race, colour, sex, language, religion, political or other opinion, national or social origin, property, birth or other status.*"

Nevertheless, this universal character is highly contended by supporters of cultural relativism. They claim that there are no universal human values and that the variety of cultures implies that human rights can, and may, be interpreted differently. In between, moderate forms of both theories exist.[5] While human rights norms have a universal character and apply to everyone on the basis of their human dignity, cultural rights are community-specific and differ from one community to another. Cultural diversity does not exist only between groups and societies; there is diversity within each group and society. Therefore, it is questionable whether cultural rights may be called 'universal'. Bhikhu Parekh rightly asserts that there are three essential conditions of multicultural societies: "cultural embeddedness of human beings, the inescapability and desirability of cultural diversity and intercultural dialogue, and the internal plurality of each culture".[6]

Cultural Rights in International Human Rights Instruments[7]

Cultural Rights in the UDHR, 1948

In order to preserve and protect the cultural identity of the multifarious groups and communities, Article 7 proclaims that all are equal before the law and are entitled without any discrimination to equal protection of the law. All are entitled to equal protection against any discrimination in violation of this Declaration and against any incitement to such discrimination. Again, Article 22 states that everyone, as a member of society, has the right to social security and is entitled to realization, through national effort and international cooperation and in accordance with the organization and resources of each State in the economic, social and cultural rights indispensable for his dignity and the free development of his personality. Right to participation in the cultural life of the community is guaranteed by Article 27.

Cultural Rights in the International Covenant on Civil and Political Rights and International Covenant on Economic, Social and Cultural Rights

Although the ICCPR deals primarily with civil and political rights, yet it also regards cultural rights as a part of civil rights. Article 18, for instance, provides that all shall have the right to freedom of thought, conscience and religion. This right shall include freedom to have or to adopt a religion or belief of his choice, and freedom, either individually or in community with others and in public or private, to manifest his religion or belief in worship, observance, practice and teaching. In those States in which ethnic, religious or linguistic minorities exist, persons belonging to such minorities shall not be denied the right, in community with the other members of their group, to enjoy their own culture, to profess and practice their own religion, or to use their own language (Article 27). Article 15 (1) of the ICSECR provides that the State Parties shall recognize the right of everyone to take part in cultural life. However, these rights could not protect the multicultural character of the population in different countries and a 'clash of civilizations' occurred in a number of countries leading to disintegration of some of the East European countries.

Universal Declaration on Cultural Diversity 2001

The General Conference of the United Nations Educational, Scientific and Cultural Organization adopted the Universal Declaration on Cultural Diversity on Nov. 2, 2001 to ensure the preservation and promotion of the fruitful diversity of cultures and simultaneously affirming that respect for the diversity of cultures, tolerance, dialogue and cooperation, in a climate of mutual trust and understanding are among the best guarantees of international peace and security.

Accommodation of cultural diversity is intrinsic to unity and integrity. This is recognized through Article 1 which states that culture takes diverse forms across time and space. This diversity is embodied in the uniqueness and plurality of the identities of the groups and societies making up humankind. However, it is not sufficient just to support pluralities; it is equally important to recognize them. Diversities should be recognized through policies of inclusion and participation for all citizens. This is the essence of multiculturalism too.

Despite the inescapability of a debate between cultural relativism and universalism, Article 4 affirms that cultural diversity and human rights are entwined. Article 4 states that the defence of cultural diversity is an ethical imperative, inseparable from respect for human dignity. No one may invoke cultural diversity to infringe upon human rights guaranteed by international law, nor to limit their scope.

Along similar lines, Article 5 - Cultural rights as an enabling environment for cultural diversity

Cultural rights are an integral part of human rights, which are universal, indivisible and interdependent. All persons should have the freedom to express themselves in their mother tongue; all persons should be entitled to quality education with full respect to their cultural identity; and all persons have the right to participate in the cultural life of their choice subject to respect for human rights and fundamental freedoms of others.

Article 6 maintains that human rights and cultural rights are universal and inalienable and everyone by virtue of being human should have access to cultural diversity. Freedom of speech and expression, multilingualism, media and art are specific means of ensuring guarantees of cultural diversity.

For true international cooperation in the cultural field Article 10 reaffirms the necessity of strengthening capacities for creation and dissemination worldwide. In the face of current imbalances in flows and exchanges of cultural goods and services at the global level, it is necessary to reinforce international cooperation and solidarity aimed at enabling all countries, especially developing countries and countries in transition, to establish cultural industries that are viable and competitive at national and international level.

Article 11 - Building partnerships between the public sector, the private sector and civil society.

Market forces alone cannot guarantee the preservation and promotion of cultural diversity, which is the key to sustainable human development. From this perspective, the pre-eminence of public policy, in partnership with the private sector and civil society, must be reaffirmed.

Article 12 - The role of UNESCO

UNESCO, by virtue of its mandate and functions, has the responsibility to:

(a) Promote the incorporation of the principles set out in the present Declaration into the development strategies drawn up within the various intergovernmental bodies;

(b) Serve as a reference point and a forum where States, international governmental and non-governmental organizations, civil society and the private sector may join together in elaborating concepts, objectives and policies in favour of cultural diversity;

(c) Pursue its activities in standard-setting, awareness-raising and capacity-building in the areas related to the present Declaration within its fields of competence;

(d) Facilitate the implementation of the Action Plan, the main lines of which are appended to the present Declaration.

Protection of Cultural Rights: Countries and Constitutions

Since most of the countries today are multilinguistic, multi-religious, multi-ethnic, statesmen and policy makers are seriously trying to address the issues relating to diversity and how to overcome them. While it is not possible to study the constitutional provisions of all the multicultural countries as part of this present study, but for the purpose of the present discussion, I would highlight some of the constitutional provisions pertaining to human rights and cultural diversity and thereby attempt a comparative analysis of them in order to reveal the position of India as a multicultural state and its policies towards its identities.

Australia

Australia, home to a number of indigenous and non-indigenous populations has been subjected to a long history of immigration. In the 2001 census, 6.7 million people identified their ancestry as Australian, 6.4 million as English, 1.9 million as Irish, while Italian, German, Chinese and Scottish each had over half a million descendents.[8] The country's ethnic population has since 1901 suffered from several exclusionary measures for instance "indigenous populations were deliberately excluded from the 1901 constitution at the Federation of the British colonies in Australia. Aborigines were not afforded citizenship rights in their own country until a 1967 referendum changed the legislation".[9] Australia responded to the problems of the diverse identities by enacting the Community Relations Commission and The Principles of Multiculturalism Act, 2000 which emphasizes that ethnicity, race, language and religion should not play any part in determining or defining the status of a citizen. So too the loyalty and commitment of a citizen to a state should not relate to the individual's race, religion, language and ethnicity. They should have the right of self-identification by way of any of those identifiers.[10]

Furthermore, Article 46 of the Australian Constitution provides that the Commonwealth shall not make any law for establishing any religion, or for imposing any religious observance, or for prohibiting the free exercise of any religion. Nonetheless, since religion falls under the residuary power of states, the states are free to legislate in religious matters. Contradictorily the preamble to the Australian Constitution uses the words, "Whereas the people of New South Wales, Victoria, South Australia, Queensland and Tasmania humbly relying on the blessing of *Almighty God* have agreed to unite" imports a reliance on the religious spirit.[11] It can be said that the essence of secularism appears to be obscured by these implications. It appears that the Constitution though striving to promote diversity has been unable till date to fully accommodate them.

Canada

"*Canada has become a post-national, multicultural society. It contains the globe within its borders, and Canadians have learnt that their two international languages and their diversity are a comparative advantage and a source of continuing creativity and innovation. Canadians are, by virtue of history and necessity, open to the world*"—the Right Honourable Jean Chretien, Prime Minister of Canada, June 2000.

Diversity has been a fundamental characteristic of Canada since its beginnings. At the time of European settlement, there were about more than 56 Aboriginal nations speaking more than 30 languages. Comprised of over 200 ethnic groups divided amongst races, languages, regions, cultures and communities represent an ideal multicultural society. Added to this is the trend towards immigration of English, French, Scottish, Irish, German, Italian, Chinese, Ukrainian and North American Indian. Religious diversity is increasing with Catholics (43% in 2001) and Protestant (29% in 2001) supplemented by significant numbers of Muslims, Hindus, Sikhs and Buddhists. The linguistic diversity is reflected by the fact that although English and French are Canada's official languages, in the 2001 census more than 100 languages were reported as a mother tongue ... the proportion of people for whom English or French is not a mother tongue has increased to 18 per cent (59% of Canadians speak English as a first language, 23 per cent speak French).[12]

To tackle the manifold diversities of races, languages and religions, Canada adopted a multicultural policy emphasizing on 'negotiated integration'. Article 27 of the Canadian Constitution proclaims that the Charter shall be interpreted in a manner consistent with the preservation and enhancement of the multicultural heritage of Canadians.[13] A broad framework of laws and policies supports Canada's approach to diversity. At the federal level, these include the Canadian Charter of Rights and Freedoms, the Canadian Human Rights Act, the Employment Equity Act, the Official Languages Act, the Pay Equity Act and the Multiculturalism Act. Provinces and territories also have laws, human rights commissions and programmes that promote diversity. Finally, Canada reinforces its commitment to diversity as a signatory to international conventions including, for example, the Universal Declaration of Human Rights and the International Covenant on Economic, Social and Cultural Rights.

However, it appears contextual to mention that making equality of opportunity meaningful in a diverse society requires more than constitutional measures and legislations. All levels of government in Canada deliver programmes that mobilize communities to promote dialogue and help people overcome barriers to their participation in society. In spite of the various policies and the Canadian Multiculturalism Act, the Canadian society are still facing problems "to deal with complex and intersecting identities".[14] This is primarily because the legislation that recognizes and protects diverse groups protects specific groups or identities making it difficult to address multiple challenges or intersections at once.[15] The Canadian Constitution has been unable to successfully resolve the problems of ethnic minorities.

China

The People's Republic of China represents a unitary multicultural country comprising of 56 ethnic groups, of these Han group constitutes 91.96 per cent of the total population and the rest 55 ethnic groups comprises the minority communities. The 1982 Constitution of People's Republic of China recognizes the nature of ethnic diversity and emphasizes that the state guarantees the language rights and interests of all ethnic groups and encourages the maintenance and development of the equality, unity and cooperative relations among all ethnic groups. Article 4 (1) of the Constitution of the People's Republic of China provides that the State protects the lawful rights and interests of the minority nationalities and upholds and develops the relationship of equality, unity and mutual assistance among all of China's nationalities.[16] Clause 2 of the same article provides that regional autonomy is practiced in areas where people of minority nationalities live in compact communities; in these areas organs of self-government are established for the exercise of the right of autonomy.[17] The Constitution also provides for linguistic autonomy in the sense that Article 4 (3) provides that the people of all nationalities have the freedom to use and develop their own spoken and written languages, and to preserve or reform their own ways and customs.[18]

Discrimination against and oppression of any ethnic group are forbidden. "Ethnic regional autonomy is a basic policy made by the government according to the special circumstances of China, and also an important political system. From 1947 to the end of 1998, China established 5 autonomous regions, 30 autonomous prefectures and 120 autonomous counties. Altogether 144 ethnic groups have set up autonomous areas at various levels and the ethnic members in ethnic autonomous areas account for 75 per cent of the total ethnic population".[19]

Nevertheless, there appears a wide gap between rhetoric and reality. Ethnic groups taking advantage of religious discrimination try to raise group consciousness and "resort to spliticism in order to establish independent states".[20] Thus in the light of separatist movements going on in Xinjiang and in other parts of the country, it cannot be said that the constitutional provisions have served to protect and promote diversity.

South Africa

South Africa, though a multicultural society, has been under the shackles of apartheid for a long time. The Constitution making process represented a historic compromise between the white regime and the liberation movements and the manner in which the different challenges facing the society were resolved.

The Preamble to the Constitution of South Africa, 1996 proclaims that "South Africa belongs to all who live in it, united in our diversity" and the founding values reflect a commitment to one sovereign democratic state founded on the values of human dignity, the achievement of equality and the advancement of human rights and freedoms amongst others.

Moreover, in order to preserve the rich linguistic diversity of the country, the African Constitution recognizes 11 official languages. The Bill of Rights guarantees equality to all. Apart from the equality provisions, the Constitution guarantees freedom of religion, belief and opinion including the recognition of personal and family law under tradition or religion. Individuals are given the freedom to participate in the cultural life of their choice. However, the rights to culture, language and religion are recognized only to the extent that they may not be exercised in any manner inconsistent with any provision in the Bill of Rights. This may be seen in some quarters as relegating them to some secondary status.

Nevertheless, a unique feature of the Constitution is that it provides for the establishment of an independent body known as the Commission for the Promotion and Protection of the Rights of Cultural, Religious and Linguistic Communities with the object in the main of promoting respect for the rights of cultural, religious and linguistic communities.

The true nature of multicultural Africa is reflected in its constitutional recognition of the 'notion of the right of self-determination of any community sharing a common cultural and language heritage' within the nation. A number of institutions have been created to provide for cultural, religious and linguistic rights to the diverse African communities. Yet in practice it appears that the different institutions of cultural accommodation seem to exclude the underclass that constitutes a significant proportion of the population. The above analysis reveals that considerable importance has been given to cultural diversity, equality and language rights. But not much has been achieved so far. There still remains a lot to be done because in reality the majority of the Africans do not actually enjoy these rights.

Switzerland

Switzerland is a small country of about 7 million inhabitants surrounded by Germany, France, Italy, Austria and the small principality of Liechtenstein. Though a small nation, it is not ethnically homogenous. It is composed of a rich diversity of different cultures and religions. In fact, multiculturalism is a challenge to Swiss federalism. Yet, the needs of the diverse entities have been successfully accommodated by the new Constitution, which contains provisions for the different cultural, linguistic and religious communities.

The recognition of Swiss multiculturalism is clearly reflected in Article 2. Paragraph 2 of the Constitution obliges the Confederation to foster the cultural diversity of the Federation. According to Thomas Fleiner, the multiculturality and the diversity of the Swiss society is the pre-constitutional reality, which is reflected in Swiss federalism.[21] He further emphasizes that "in order to respond to these necessities the Federal Constitution did establish political institutions and procedures, which enable a peaceful settlement and management of internal conflicts."[22]

Moreover, Article 50 of the Constitution provides for the free exercise of religion within limits compatible with public order and morality. The 1998 Constitution under Article 15 provides for the 'fundamental freedom of religion and conscience' (or 'philosophy') for the person to choose his or her religion, ideology alone or together in a community for the performance of religious activities.[23] Apart from guaranteeing religious freedom, the Constitution also promotes linguistic diversity by recognizing German, French, Italian and Romansh as the national languages of the Confederation. (Article 4 of the 1998 Constitution). Although the new

Constitution, does not specify by elaborate provisions, the language freedoms of the people, but, Harihar Bhattacharyya after an extensive study of the Swiss constitutional system, opined that "language freedoms get qualified and modified at the Cantonal, and often at the Communal, levels which decide, on the basis of territoriality principle, the exact status of a language for educational and official purposes".[24]

Nonetheless, both the old and the new Constitution do not contain any provision guaranteeing equal opportunities to the people. It guarantees equal rights and the "right to be equal" as part of a minority the same value.[25] He argues that

> "If persons belonging to the Romansh minority have only equal rights, they will always be considered or they will consider themselves as second class citizens. In a totally equal society, they remain a tiny minority, which feels *de facto* discriminated in a state, which reduces the citizen to an only political person naked of any culture. If they have on the other hand the right to be equal, they must be accepted on equal terms as being part of their cultural community. A Romansh speaking citizen needs to have the same value as part of his community just in the same way as persons belonging to the majority of the German speaking community. It is obvious that Switzerland is seeking a balance between equal individual rights and the right to be respected as equal although belonging to a minority. "[26]

Apart from the afore-mentioned provisions federalism also contributed to the cause of conflict-management. The Cantons, which represent the political units, enjoy some sovereign power and the people of the cantons are politically committed to their Canton and their federation, culturally they are linked to the strong culture of their related people of the neighbour country. Harihar Bhattacharyya, here, contends that "the multilayered character of Swiss identity is both political and cultural. At the federal level, it is more political than at Cantonal and Communal levels where it is more cultural than political".[27] The multiculturalists strongly contend that had the Swiss Constitution not taken this reality into account, today Switzerland would have been disintegrated into different ethnic communities. In fact, the new Constitution upholds the principles of federalism and diversity to be the best guarantee of Swiss multiculturalism.

India

Instead of discouraging differences, the Constitution of India takes them for granted and offers adequate facilities for their expression and development. On the occasion of the 50th Anniversary of the first sitting of the Constituent Assembly, the then President Dr. Shankar Dayal Sharma stated:

> "There was a sense of mission in the members of the Constituent Assembly to draft a Constitution which would preserve the pluralism and essential oneness, and the unity and integrity of India. ... We have provided flesh and blood to the constitutional edifice bequeathed to us by the founding fathers. ...If we look at nations around us, we can be proud of our resilient, living Constitution which has adapted over time, to changing circumstances, needs and requirements. Indeed, it has become a model for constitutions in other countries. ...we must all comprehend the importance of unity, the true significance of the canons of propriety and the value of having the freedom to voice different viewpoints which, indeed, are the hallmarks of any pluralistic society. As our sages of yore said, our aims are common, our endeavours common, and there are diverse ways to reach our goal."[28]

The Report of the National Commission to Review the Working of the Constitution, 2000, too emphasized that "the framers of the Constitution sought to unite this vast country with its great diversity and many languages and creeds with the common bond of constitutional justice on the great ideals of Justice, Liberty, Equality and Fraternity ... They made a bold attempt to base the constitutional foundations on the firm faith that all classes of people, followers of all faiths and particularly the traditionally under-privileged should all join to work for their united constitutional salvation on the shared faith that the peoples as a whole must sink or swim together and that in the long run prosperity and salvation are in union and not in division."[29]

Part III of the Constitution entitled 'Fundamental Rights' provides for six categories of rights inclusive of individual and collective rights. Article 14 provides for equality before law, a provision found in almost all the countries of the world. Gurpreet Mahajan opines that "what was distinctive in the approach that India adopted at this time was that it *linked equality for the individual with equality for diverse communities*. Thus, human rights were entwined with cultural rights. It began with the understanding that equality for individuals required that different communities within the polity should exist as equals. ...It was felt that respect for the individual requires respect for the diverse beliefs and ways of life that these persons embody. Besides, the individual could not possibly exist as an equal if the community to which he or she belongs were disadvantaged or marginalized in the public domain".[30] For the fulfillment of this end Article 15(1) provides that the State shall not discriminate against any citizen on grounds only of religion, race, caste, sex, place of birth or any of them. Article 16(2) provides that no citizen shall on grounds only of religion, race, caste, sex, descent, place of birth, residence or any of them, be eligible for, or discriminated against in respect of, any employment or office under the State. Further, Article 16(5) provides that a law may prescribe that "the incumbent of an office in connection with the affairs of any religious or denominational institution, or any member of the governing body thereof, shall be a person professing a particular religion or belonging to a particular denomination." India being a land of diversities, the framers incorporated these articles specifically to prevent the majoritarian influence over minorities.

Minority Provisions

India has a composite population having a number of groups based on religion, language, caste or backwardness, such as, the Scheduled Castes, Scheduled Tribes, Anglo Indians, Muslims, Parsis, Sikhs, and Indian Christians etc.[31] The framers of the Constitution deliberated upon the ways to safeguard the interests of the minorities and protect them from all forms of discrimination and thereby enable them to get themselves integrated in mainstream national life.[32] Towards this end Articles 29 and 30 provide certain cultural and educational rights to the minorities. These two provisions owe its origin to the Constitution of Burma and the Irish Republic. Article 29(1) says that any section of the citizens residing in the territory of India having a distinct language, script or culture of its own shall have the right to conserve the same. This means that if a cultural minority wants to preserve its own language and culture, the state cannot by law impose on it any other culture belonging to the local majority. In fact, the framers of the Constitution gave protection to both the religious and linguistic minorities through this provision. Further, Article 29(2) forbids any discrimination against any citizen on the basis of religion, race, caste or language in the matter of admission into educational institutions maintained or aided by the state.

Again, Article 30 (1) says that all minorities, whether based on religion, or language, shall have the right to establish and administer educational institutions of their choice. The minorities whether based on religion or language quite understandably regard it as essential that the education of their children should be in accordance with the teachings of their religion, and they hold, quite honestly, that such an education cannot be obtained in ordinary schools designed for all the members of the public but can only be secured in schools conducted under the influence and guidance of people well-versed in the tenets of their religion and in the traditions of their culture".[33] In line with this process of thought, further, Article 30 (2) says that the State shall not, in granting aid to educational institutions discriminate against any educational institution on the ground that it is under the management of a minority, whether based on religion or language. This article fulfills two objectives at the same time—the purpose of conserving their religion language or culture, also the purpose of giving general education to their children.

Furthermore, to protect the interests of the minorities, seats are to be reserved for the Scheduled Castes and Scheduled Tribes in Lok Sabha (Article 330) and in the State Legislative Assemblies (Article 332). Originally this reservation was to operate for 10 years from the commencement of the Constitution. But this duration has been extended continuously since then by 10 years each time. Provisions have been made for the setting up of Tribal Advisory Councils and separate departments in the States and the appointments of a Special officer at the Centre to promote their welfare and safeguard their interests (Articles 164 and 338 and Fifth Schedule of the constitution). Again, under Article 339 (1) President may appoint a Commission at any time, and must appoint it after 10 years of the commencement of the constitution, to report on the welfare of the Scheduled Tribes in States and the administration of the Scheduled Areas. For the protection of the Scheduled Tribes and the prevention of atrocities, Parliament has enacted the Scheduled Castes and the Scheduled Tribes (Prevention of Atrocities) Act, 1989.

Apart from the Scheduled Castes and Scheduled Tribes, constitution also contains special provisions for the protection of the interest of Anglo-Indians who constitute a religious, social and linguistic minority. If the President is of the opinion that the Anglo-Indian community is not adequately represented in the Lok Sabha, he may nominate 2 members to the Lok Sabha (Article 331). Similarly, the Governor may nominate 1 member of the Anglo-Indian community to the State Legislative Assembly, if he is of the opinion that the Anglo-Indian community is not adequately represented.

The constitution also defines a positive, directional role for the state in this respect. It directs every state (federal unit) to provide adequate facilities for instruction in the mother-tongue at the primary stage of education of children belonging to linguistic minority groups, and empowers the President to issue proper direction to any state (Article 350A). These provisions are not just false promises. The executive has established elaborate enforcement mechanisms. After the Mondal Commission case the Supreme Court provided for the establishment of an agency for monitoring the applicability of these constitutional directives. As such the National Commission for Minorities Act (1992) was passed by Parliament in 1992 to monitor the working of the constitutional safeguards in Union and state laws. It not only provides scope for protection of minority interests but seeks to ensure that individuals belonging to minority groups do not suffer from discrimination.

The purpose of all these aforesaid provisions "is to integrate the minorities into one mainstream of national life and thus keep in check the divisive forces which may otherwise be released by the existence of several minority groups".[34]

Linguistic Diversity

Language is considered to be the most noteworthy facet of culture in determining ethnicity. Linguistic homogeneity acts as a binding force in multicultural countries, albeit, it can equally be a divisive force as is evident in the breaking away of east Pakistan (now Bangladesh) wherein Urdu was imposed on the Bengali population of east Pakistan; Sri Lanka is also sharply divided between the Tamil and the Sinhalese speakers; Belgium, between the French and Flemish speaking populations.

In order to give due recognition to the different linguistic entities as many as twenty-two languages have been 'officially' recognized and placed under the Eighth Schedule of the Indian Constitution. In addition to this, English is given the status of an associate official language till the time the people of non-Hindi speaking regions are prepared to accept Hindi. Hindi has already been recognized as the language for inter-state communication that is link language, in our Constitution. Accordingly, Article 343 provides that the official language of the Union shall be Hindi in Devanagri script. Further, Article 351 of the Indian Constitution reads: "It shall be the duty of the Union to promote the spread of the Hindi language, to develop it so that it may serve as a medium of expression for all the elements of the composite culture of India and to secure its enrichment by assimilating without interfering with its genius, the forms, style and expressions, used in Hindustani and in other languages of India specified in the Eighth Schedule, and by drawing, wherever necessary or desirable, for its vocabulary, primarily on Sanskrit and secondarily on other languages".[35] Further, Article 345 provides that every State Legislature is empowered to adopt anyone or more of the languages in use in the State for all or any of the official purposes of the State concerned. Moreover, in order to protect the interests of the linguistic communities, the Constitution has incorporated Article 347, whereby the President is empowered to direct a state Government to recognize a particular language for official purposes either for the whole or a part of the State, if he is satisfied, on a representation made to him in this regard, that a substantial proportion of the population of the State desires such recognition. This provision provides ample scope of promotion and enhancement of languages of the different communities. Again, there is Article 350 which provides that every person is entitled to submit a representation for the redress of any grievance to any officer or authority of the Union or a State in any of the languages used in the Union or in the State, as the case may be. Similarly, Articles 210 and 120 of the Constitution provides that the business of the Parliament of State Legislature will be transacted in the language of the State or in English or Hindi but if a Legislator is unable to express himself in the afore-mentioned languages then he can communicate in his mother-tongue.

Religious Pluralism

India being a land of numerous religions, the Constitution grants the citizens right to profess, practice and propagate any religion. However, one unique feature of Indian Constitution is the right to propagate one's religion (Art. 25). Many Constitutions grant a right to their citizens to practice and profess any religion, but it is a major contribution of Indian Constitution that it grants, in addition, the right to, propagate religion but cannot force someone into converting into another religion.[36] This is a unique and a novel feature. Actually Article 25 seeks to embody the principles of religious tolerance and serve to emphasize the secular nature of Indian democracy which the founding fathers considered should be the very basis of the Constitution.

Religious communities also have the right to set up their own religious and charitable institutions; they can establish their own educational institutions, and above all, these institutions can receive financial support from the state. Taken together, these are ways by which rights of diverse communities are promoted.

It would not be wrong to state that the framers gave these rights in order to enable the different religious, linguistic, ethnic and other minorities to maintain their individuality as well as distinct identity of their language and culture. The Constitution not only provides for rights but also provides for certain duties to be followed by the citizens to enable them to enjoy the rights. Part IV-A of the Constitution entitled Fundamental Duties consists of eleven duties to be observed by the citizens. Article 51A (e) provides that it shall be the duty of every citizen of India to promote harmony and the spirit of common brotherhood amongst all the people of India transcending religious, linguistic and regional or sectional diversities; and Article 51A (f) to value and preserve the rich heritage of our composite culture. It is these two provisions which entrusts the citizens with a sacred obligation that of preserving diversity at all costs.

Jawaharlal Nehru in *India Today and Tomorrow* categorically emphasized that "India is a common home for all those who live here; to whatever religion they may belong [...] they have equal rights and obligations. Ours is a composite Nation." This composite character is also well reflected through the different provisions.

The auspicious work of promoting human rights started by the UN sixty years ago has been the guiding force of all the documents and Charters of this world body. This has become all the more relevant in this contemporary world tormented by ethnic, religious and racial conflicts. Furthermore, there is the added problem of protecting minority rights from the dominance of the majorities not only in the developing countries but also in the developed world since ninety five per cent of the people live in multicultural societies. "Fifty-five years, the Universal Declaration of Human Rights gave us a universal, indivisible, holistic framework of values and principles which reiterate and reverberate core concepts of equality, non-discrimination, participation, accountability, well-being and justice for all".[37] In consonance with these principles some of the States have taken a positive mechanism for the protection of cultural diversity. However, there are a great majority of countries which have resorted to forced integration, assimilation, discrimination, ethnic cleansing, despite being signatories to major Conventions. Effective protection of the human rights of minorities and different multicultural groups requires a creative interplay between mechanisms at the international and regional levels and those at the national level. It needs to be emphasized that human rights would remain a distant dream until these communities are allowed a democratic environment of equality and recognition.

Notes

1. S.P. Huntington, *The Clash of Civilizations and the Remaking of World Order*, Simon and Schuster, New York, 1996, p. 21.
2. Statement by a group of United Nations experts on the World Day for Cultural Diversity for Dialogue and Development, 21 May, 2010.
3. Bhikhu Parekh, *Rethinking Multiculturalism, Cultural Diversity and Political Theory*, Palgrave, New York, 2000, p. 143.
4. *Ibid*, p. 167.
5. Yvonne Donders, *Do cultural diversity and human rights make a good match*, UNESCO, 2010.
6. Bhikhu Parekh, *Rethinking Multiculturalism, Cultural Diversity and Political Theory*, Palgrave, New York, 2000, p. 338.
7. Among which, in particular, the Florence Agreement of 1950 and its Nairobi Protocol of 1976, the Universal Copyright Convention of 1952, the Declaration of Principles on International Cultural Co-operation of 1966, the Convention on the Means of Prohibiting and Preventing the Illicit Import, Export and Transfer of Ownership of Cultural Property (1970), the Convention for the Protection of World Cultural and Natural Heritage of 1972, the UNESCO Declaration on Race

and Racial Prejudice of 1978, the Recommendation concerning the Status of the Artist of 1980, and the Recommendation on Safeguarding Traditional and Popular Culture of 1989.

8. Stepan Kerkyasharian, "Multiculturalism in Australia: Finding or Losing Our Way", in *Canadian Diversity*, Vol. 4, No.1, Winter 2005, p. 110.
9. *Ibid.*
10. *Ibid.*
11. Ryan, "Constitution of Commonwealth of Australia", p. 380 in L.M.Singhvi, *Constitution of India,* Vol. 1, Modern Law Publications, New Delhi, 2006, p. 51.
12. John Biles, Eriin Tolley and Humera Ibrahim, "Does Canada have a Multicultural Future?" *Canadian Diversity*, Vol. 4, No.1, Winter 2005, p. 24.
13. M.V. Pylee, *Constitutions of the World*, Universal Law Publishing Co. Pvt. Ltd., Delhi, 2003, p. 332.
14. John Biles, Eriin Tolley and Humera Ibrahim, "Does Canada have a Multicultural Future?" *Canadian Diversity*, Vol. 4, No.1, Winter 2005, p. 27.
15. *Ibid.*
16. M.V. Pylee, *Constitutions of the World*, Universal Law Publishing Co. Pvt. Ltd., Delhi, 2003, p. 343.
17. *Ibid.*
18. *Ibid.*
19. Bing Wang, Multiculturalism in China, *Canadian Diversity*, Vol. 4, No.1, Winter 2005, p. 37.
20. *Ibid.*
21. Thomas Fleiner, *Switzerland: subsidiarity, ethnic and cultural diversity*, in the Conference "Federalism: Russian and Swiss Perspectives", June 22-23, 2001.
22. *Ibid.*
23. Harihar Bhattacharyya, *India as a Multicultural Federation, Asian Values, Democracy and Decentralization (in comparison with Swiss Federalism)*, Institute of Federalism, Fribourg, 2001, p. 323.
24. *Ibid.*, p. 313.
25. Thomas Fleiner, *Switzerland: subsidiarity, ethnic and cultural diversity*, in the Conference "Federalism: Russian and Swiss Perspectives", June 22-23, 2001.http://www.federalmeart.ksu.ru/conference/konfer3/flajner.htm
26. *Ibid.*
27. Harihar Bhattacharyya, *India as a Multicultural Federation, Asian Values, Democracy and Decentralization (in comparison with Swiss Federalism)*, Institute of Federalism, Fribourg, 2001, p. 329.

28. Address by the former President, Dr. S.D. Sharma, Parliament House, New Delhi, Monday, Dec. 9, 1996.
29. Report of the National Commission to Review the Working of the Constitution, in S.C. Kashyap, *Constitution-Making Since 1950— An Overview,* Universal Law Publishing Co. Pvt. Ltd., New Delhi, 2004, pp. 290-291
30. Gurpreet Mahajan, Negotiating Cultural Diversity and Minority Rights in India, http://www.idea.int/publications/dchs/upload/dchs_vol2_sec3_4pdf
31. M.P. Jain, *Indian Constitutional Law*, Wadhwa and Company, Nagpur, 2004, p. 1397.
32. Elaborate discussions were held in the Constituent Assembly, Constituent Assembly Debates, Vol. III, pp. 211-314.
33. L.M. Singhvi, *Constitution of India*, Vol. 2, Modern Law Publications, New Delhi, 2006, p. 1319.
34. M.P. Jain, *Indian Constitutional Law*, Wadhwa and Company, Nagpur, 2004, p. 1399.
35. P. M. Bakshi, *The Constitution of India*, Universal Law Publishing Co. Pvt. Ltd., 2003, p. 290.
36. Akhtar Majeed, "Federalism, Decentralization and Conflict-Management in Multicultural Societies", in *Federations*, Special Triple Issue: Themes of the International Conference on Federalism, 2002, p. 22.
37. C.J. Dias, "Democracy and Human Rights: The Challenge of Ethnicity and Inclusive Democracy", *Journal of Indian Law Institute*, 2005, p. 12.

7

Environment and Human Rights

Climate change, destruction of the ozone layer, desertification, fresh water shortages, etc. the list of current environmental problems, which are assuming ever more menacing dimensions, seems endless. The present state of our environment is distressing. All-over the world, people are witnessing the undesirable effects of environmental decline, from flash floods to fish kills to landslides on deforested slopes, global warming and ultimately everything affects the human lifestyle. "Despite the evident relationship between environmental degradation and human suffering, human rights violations and environmental degradation have been treated by most organizations and governments as unrelated issues. Just as human rights activists have laid emphasis only on civil and political rights onto their agendas, environmentalists have tended to focus primarily on common property resources and sustainable development without addressing human impacts of environmental abuse. As a result, victims of environmental degradation are unguarded by the laws and mechanisms established to address human rights abuses".[1] How can the existence of individual rights be reconciled with the rules on environmental protection, which is in the interest of the whole community?

Environment and Human Rights: The Linkage

Environment and human rights have traditionally been envisaged as two distinct, independent spheres of rights. However, it was precisely towards the end of the twentieth century, that concern was expressed that human rights may play a role in environmental protection.

Nevertheless, scholars are not unanimous regarding the complex issues that may arise when these two seemingly distinct spheres interact, and this has given rise to three approaches on 'human rights and the environment'.[2]

The first approach emphasizes that a quality environment is a precondition for enjoying human rights. Environmental law is conceptualized as 'giving a protection that would help ensure the well-being of future generations as well as the survival of those who depend immediately upon natural resources for their livelihood.' The second approach focuses on the need for procedural rights of the people in relation to control over their environment. Procedural human rights such as access to information, access to justice and participation in political decision-making are often crucial for ensuring policies that respect environmental concerns. The third approach expresses the crucial need for a substantially justiceable right to a quality environment. There has been a simultaneous increase in 'legal claims for both human rights and environmental goods,' which is a clear reflection of the link between 'human' and the 'environment' and the dependence of human life on the environment. Thus, the right to a healthy environment is a fundamental part of the right to life and personal liberty.

United Nations and Protection of Environment

Since its inception, the UN has established itself as "the most significant political embodiment of the international community".[3] Article 55 of the Charter requires the UN to promote, firstly, higher standards of living, full employment, and conditions of economic and social progress and development, secondly, solutions to international economic, social, health and related problems, and thirdly, observance of human rights and fundamental freedoms. These principles can be fulfilled only in the presence of a pollution free wholesome environment.

The International Covenant on Civil and Political Rights (ICCPR) contains provisions related either directly or indirectly to environment.

Article 1: The right of "all peoples to freely dispose of their natural wealth and resources" and the prohibition against States' depriving a people of its means of subsistence;

Article 11: The right to an adequate standard of living, including adequate food and housing;

Article 12: The right to the highest attainable standard of health.

In accordance with these principles, the UN Environment Programme (UNEP) was established in 1972 and the Commission on Sustainable Development (CSD) in 1992. The United Nations strongly acknowledged that a healthy environment was essential for the recognition and enjoyment of human rights and fundamental freedoms. In 1997, the Commission on Human Rights appointed a Special Rapporteur to study the "adverse effects of the illicit movement and dumping of toxic and dangerous products and wastes on the enjoyment of human rights".[4] Further, the Commission on Human Rights in its decision 2001/111 emphasized the need to organize a joint expert seminar "to review and assess progress achieved since the United Nations Conference on Environment and Development in promoting and protecting human rights in relation to environmental questions and in the framework of Agenda 21".[5]

Principle 10 of the Rio Declaration on Environment and Development of 1992 established the fact that human rights and environment were closely related:

> "Environmental issues are best handled with the participation of all concerned citizens, at the relevant level. At the national level, each individual shall have appropriate access to information concerning the environment that is held by public authorities, including the information on hazardous materials and activities in their communities, and the opportunity to participate in decision making

> processes. States shall facilitate and encourage public awareness and participation by making information widely available. Effective access to judicial and administrative proceedings, including redress and remedy, shall be provided".[6]

It is interesting to refer to a rather recent initiative at the OAS level which, in justifying the interest of the organization in exploring the link between human rights and the environment, refers to a wide range of rights to be examined in the sections below. Resolution 1819 of the General Assembly of the OAS of June 2001 asserts, among other things, that the effective enjoyment of all human rights, including the right to education and the rights of assembly and freedom of expression, as well as full enjoyment of economic, social, and cultural rights, could foster better environmental protection by creating conditions conducive to modification of behaviour patterns that lead to environmental degradation, reduction of the environmental impact of poverty and of patterns of unsustainable development, more effective dissemination of information on this issue, and more active participation in political processes by groups affected by the problem [...][7]

Ultimately, statements of lofty resolutions are not enough. It is the responsibility of all the Member States of the UN to incorporate environmental consciousness into the UN human rights task. It is the joint responsibility of all the Member States of the United Nations to promote sincerely the cause of ecological protection, rights of the masses and thereby make the world a better place to live in.

Global Environmental Concern

At the international level, the first initiative in the matter of environment was taken by the Stockholm Conference of 1972. It initiated a new era in the field of environment management by establishing a link between human rights and environmental protection and emphasizing on the fact that man has a 'fundamental right to freedom, equality and adequate conditions of life, in an environment of a quality that permits a life of dignity and well-being, and he bears a solemn responsibility to protect and improve the environment for present and future generations'. As an outcome of the Conference, the United Nations Environment Programme (UNEP) was established. Almost twenty years later, in resolution 45/94, the UN General Assembly recalled the language of Stockholm, stating that all individuals are entitled to live in an environment adequate for their health and well-being. The resolution called for enhanced efforts towards ensuring a better and healthier environment.

This was followed by the United Nations Conference on Environment and Development (UNCED) also as 'the Earth Summit' in 1992 in Brazil. This programme categorically emphasized the necessity of sustainable development to ensure the health and well-being of human beings.

This was subsequently affirmed by the Vienna Declaration and Programme of Action (1993) which recognized the imperative of protecting and preserving the environment for the well-being of the present and future generations. "The World Conference on Human Rights recognized that illicit dumping of toxic and dangerous substances and waste potentially constitutes a serious threat to the human rights to life and death of everyone. Consequently, the World Conference called on all States to adopt and vigorously implement the existing conventions relating to them".[8]

To create further awareness among the State Parties, the World Summit on Sustainable Development (WSSD) was held in Johannesburg, South Africa, September, 2002. The Plan stressed the necessity of concerted effort at the national level for successful human development. The Meetings of Experts on Human Rights and the Environment (14-15 Jan., 2002) preparatory to the Seminar (16 Jan., 2002) held at Geneva to assess the progress since the 1992 Conference, concluded that the "developments indicate the close linkage between the protection of human rights and environmental protection in the context of sustainable development, the growing interrelationship between approaches to each of them, as well as the synergies that have developed between these previously distinct fields".[9]

Apart from the efforts by the UN, it is noteworthy that some of the regional human rights enforcement agencies, too, stressed the importance of healthy environment for the fulfillment of human rights. Mention may be made of the (1) African Charter on Human and Peoples Rights, (2) African Commission on Human and Peoples Rights, and (3) Protocol of San Salvador to the American Convention.

Regional Concerns

In consonance with the resolutions of the Stockholm Conference a number of regional bodies have been formed to promote the cause of environmental human rights. Article 11 of the Additional Protocol to the Inter-American Convention on Human Rights (1994) popularly known as the San Salvador Protocol, states that (1) everyone shall have the right to live in a healthy environment and to have access to basic public services; (2) the state parties shall promote the protection, preservation and improvement of the environment. The Convention on the Rights of the Child (1989) at Article 24(2) (c) requires State parties in the matter of combating disease and malnutrition to take into consideration, 'the damage and risks of environmental pollution.' The African Charter on Human and People's Rights, 1981 proclaims in Art. 24(1) the right to 'a general satisfactory environment favourable to their development.' In fact, the Final Report of the Special Rapporteur on Prevention of Discrimination and Protection of Minorities[10] listed over 15 rights relative to environmental quality. Some of these include:

(a) the right to freedom from pollution, environmental degradation and activities which threaten life, health or livelihood;
(b) protection and preservation of the air, soil, water, flora and fauna;

(c) healthy food and water; a safe and healthy working environment.

Links between the environment and human rights have also been recognized by the Inter-American Court of Human Rights. The construction of a highway was found to have violated the American Declaration of the Rights and Duties of Man. Similarly, the Commission established a link between environmental quality and the right to life in response to a petition brought on behalf of the Yanomani Indians of Brazil.[11]

The Constitution of India and Environmental Human Rights

An individual right to environmental protection has been recognized in a number of constitutions: Belgium (Art. 23-4), Hungary[12], Norway (Art. 110, b), Poland (Art. 71), Portugal (Art. 66-2), Slovakia (Art. 44 & 45), Slovenia (Art. 72 & 73), Spain (Art. 45-1) and Turkey (Art. 56). Protection of the environment is included as a so-called "state objective"[13] in the constitutions of Austria (Art. 10-12), Finland (Art. 20), Germany (Art. 20, a), Greece (Art. 24), Netherlands (Art. 21), Sweden (Art. 2-2) and Switzerland (Art. 24-7).

Originally, the Constitution of India did not contain any specific provision relating to environmental protection. But keeping in view of the International Conference on Human Environment at Stockholm in 1972 of which India was a signatory and the growing awareness for ecological degradation, the Indian Parliament passed the Forty-second Constitution Amendment Act, 1976 which incorporated two significant articles: Articles 48-A and 51-A (g) to protect and conserve the environment. In addition, it also introduced certain changes in the Seventh Schedule of the Constitution.

> Article 48-A: "The State shall endeavour to protect and improve the environment and to safeguard the forests and wildlife of the country".
>
> Article 51- A (g): "It shall be the duty of every citizen of India... (g) to protect and improve the natural

environment including forests, lakes and wildlife and to have compassion for living creatures".

Schedule Seven: List III, Concurrent List
Item No. 17-A: Forests
17-B: Protection of Wild Animals and Birds
20-A: Population Control and Family Planning.

Thus, various entries of State List II were transferred to List III (Concurrent List) which empowered Parliament to legislate on environmental issues such as forests, wildlife, population control, family planning etc.

Fundamental Rights

Part III of the Indian Constitution, entitled Fundamental Rights does not contain any specific provision relating to environment. However, the different judicial pronouncements of the Supreme Court and High Court has significantly contributed towards giving a new dimension to environmental protection in the form of newer and newer interpretations of Articles 14 and 21 of the Constitution.

Right to Equality and Environment

The Indian Constitution guarantees the right to equality to all the persons without any discrimination. This indicates that any action of the 'State' relating to environment must not infringe upon the right to equality as enshrined in Article 14 of the Constitution.[14] The courts in India, on a number of occasions have struck down the arbitrary official sanction in environmental matters that it was violative of Right to Equality (Article 14). The Supreme Court has maintained that in matters of environment public interest was supreme 'because sometimes arbitrary grant of lease and indiscriminate operation of mines may jeopardize the wildlife and natural wealth of the nation'.[15]

Right to Life and Right to Clean Environment

Article 21 of the Constitution guarantees the right to life and personal liberty. The word 'life' has been interpreted by the Court to include right to live in a healthy and pollution free environment. The different judicial pronouncements have strengthened the United Nations and constitutional mandate of protecting the environment.

In Tarun Bharat Singh, Alwar v. Union of India, 1992, otherwise known as the Sariska case, the Supreme Court viewed its constitutional role as:

> "This litigation concerns environment. A great American judge emphasizing the imperative issue of environment said that he placed Government above big business, individual liberty above Government and environment above all. The issues and concerns in this case far transcend the trivialities and inhibitions of an adversarial litigation. All the parties must be forthcoming in a concerted effort to find a satisfying solution to the problem which, in more ways than one, is typical of the Indian predicament. We are, therefore, entitled to expect that the State Government and the mining entrepreneurs in their own enlightened self-interest will discard the adversarial litigative stance. The issues of environment must and shall receive the highest attention from this court".[16]

Divan and Rosencranz has brilliantly summarized the fundamental norms adopted by the court to regulate 'environmental jurisprudence'. They are as follows:

- Every person enjoys a right to a wholesome environment which is a facet of the right to life guaranteed under Article 21 of the Indian Constitution.[17]
- Enforcement agencies are under an obligation to strictly enforce environmental laws.[18]

- Government agencies may not plead non-availability of funds, inadequacy of staff or other insufficiencies to justify the non-performance of their obligations under environmental laws.[19]
- The 'polluter pays' principle which is a part of the basic environmental law of the land requires that a polluter bear the remedial or clean up costs as well as the amounts payable to compensate the victims of pollution.[20]
- The 'precautionary principle' requires government authorities to anticipate, prevent and attack the causes of environmental pollution. This principle also imposes the onus of proof on the developer or industrialist to show that his or her action is environmentally benign.[21]
- The Government development agencies charged with decision making ought to give due regard to ecological factors including the environmental policy of the Central and State Government; the sustainable development and utilization of natural resources; and
- The obligation of the present generation to preserve natural resources and pass onto future generations an environment as intact as the one we inherited from the previous generation.[22]

The State is the trustee of all natural resources which are by nature meant for public use and enjoyment. The public at large is the beneficiary of the sea-shore, running waters, air, forests and ecologically fragile lands. These resources cannot be converted into private ownership.[23]

Directive Principles of State Policy

Articles 36 to 51 of the Constitution of India deals with the Directive Principles of State Policy. Though the Directive Principles are not legally enforceable, yet they are 'fundamental in the governance of the country' and it shall be the duty of the State to apply these principles in making laws. (Article 37) Moreover, the directives are increasingly being regarded by the judiciary as supplementary and complementary to fundamental rights. Article 48-A provides that The State shall endeavour to protect and improve the environment and to safeguard the forests and wildlife of the country.

Justice Chinnappa Reddy in Sachidanand Pandey V. State of West Bengal (1987) 2 SCC 295 explained, "Whenever a problem of ecology is brought before the Court, the Court is bound to bear in mind Article 48-A of the Constitution ... and Article 51 (A) (g) which proclaims it to be the fundamental duty of every citizen of India 'to protect and improve the natural environment including forests, lakes and wildlife and to have compassion for living creatures." In Consumer Education and Research Centre V. Union of India, 1995 3 SCC 42, the Supreme Court declared that right to health, medical aid to protect health and vigour of women is a fundamental right, if Article 21 is read with Articles 39 (e), 41, 43 and 48-A. Thus, the life of a workman becomes meaningful and purposeful with dignity of person.

Fundamental Duties

In the face of growing ecological degradation and in consonance with the Stockholm declaration, the Parliament enacted the forty-second Constitution Amendment Act, 1976, which inserted Article 48-A and 51 (A) (g) which imposes an obligation upon the citizens to safeguard environment. The Supreme Court in Rural Litigation and Entitlement Kendra, Dehradun V. State of Uttar Pradesh, 1986 Supp. SCC 517, clarified that protection of environment is not only the duty of policy makers; it is as well a social obligation to be fulfilled sincerely by the citizens.

C.M. Jariwala, one of the pioneers in the field of environmental jurisprudence, has rightly observed that Articles 48-A and 51 (A) (g) reflect the "principle of intergenerational equity and various pronouncements made by the Supreme Court envisage an emergence of a right of the unborns".[24] This right to intergenerational equity and right of unborn to clean environment has emerged from Articles 21, 48-A, 51-A (g), and that "existing generation was ordained not to plunder but use nature according to one's capacity to repay".[25]

Conclusion

The protection of global environment is a common task, requiring united and cooperative action of human being as a whole residing on the earth. "Along with social progress and the advance of production, science and technology, the capability of mankind to improve the environment should increase with each passing day".[26] Therefore, what entails is a systematic and concerted action. Attainment of this goal requires concerted action on the part of citizens, communities, institutions and organizations. It cannot be denied that development is a necessity as long as it ensures sustainable development. Ecological balance has to be maintained at all costs and it is only then that environmental justice and healthy life can be attained.

A Native American proverb states that *we do not inherit the planet from our ancestors but borrow it from our children.* For this purpose, world peace is, of course, a prerequisite. It is also essential for the developed and developing countries to cooperate with the recognition that the protection of environment and the socio-economic developments are fundamentally interrelated. The process of efficient environmental engineering is not the sole responsibility of the developing countries only. Rather it should be seen that the developed nations too should conscientiously preserve the resources and at the same time protect the present and the future generations from ecological disaster. The future of the global environment does not allow optimism, but efforts towards a constructive solution must be made through worldwide cooperation rather than simply regarding the problem with pessimism.

The advancement of the relationship between human rights and the environment would enable the incorporation of human rights principles within an environmental dimension, such as anti-discrimination standards, the need for social participation and the protection of vulnerable groups. At the same time, the human rights system would be strengthened by the incorporation of environmental concerns, enabling the expansion of the scope of human rights protection and generation of concrete solutions for cases of abuses. Of course, one of the most important consequences is to provide the sufferers of environmental degradation, the opportunity to get justice from the appropriate authorities. Given the vulnerable condition of the victims of environmental degradation, linking human rights and the environment brings such victims closer to the mechanisms of protection that are provided for by human rights law. It is essential that our policies and practises should reflect our concern for the protection of both.

Notes

1. Romina Picolotti; Jorge Daniel Taillant, *Linking Human Rights and the Environment, the* Arizona University Press, 2010, http://www.uapress.arizona.edu/Books/bid1492.htm
2. Christopher Holmes, *The New Future of Human Rights and Environment: Moving the Global Agenda Forward—High Level Experts Meeting*, in http://www.iisd.ca/mea-1/guestarticle87.html
3. P.W. Birnie and A.E.Boyle, *International Law and the Environment*, Oxford University Press, New Delhi, 2004, p. 47.
4. D.R. Kaarthikeyan, "Environment and Human Rights", *International Journal of Environmental Consumerism*, Vol. 1, Issue 1, 2005, p. 85
5. *Ibid.*, p. 85.
6. *Ibid.*, p. 85.
7. http://www.unhchr.ch/environment/bp3.html
8. J.S. Verma, *The New Universe of Human Rights*, Universal Law Publishing Co. Pvt. Ltd., Delhi, 2004, p. 165.
9. *Ibid.*, p. 165.
10. http://supremecourtofindia.nic.in/new_links/humanrights.htm
11. *Ibid.*,
12. http://assembly.coe.int/Documents/WorkingDocs/doc03/EDOC9791.htm#P160_19930
13. http://assembly.coe.int/Documents/WorkingDocs/doc03/EDOC9791.htm#P161_20246
14. S.C. Shastri, *Environmental Law in India*, Eastern Book Company, Lucknow, 2005, p. 42.
15. *Ibid.*, p. 42.

16. S. Divan and A. Rosencranz, *Environmental Law and Policy in India*, Oxford University Press, New Delhi, 2004, p. 41.
17. M.C. *Mehta v. Union of India*, 1992 (3) SCC 256, 257.
18. *Indian Council for Enviro-Legal Action v. Union of India*, 1996 (5) SCC 281, 294, 301.
19. *Dr. B.L. Wadehra v. Union of India*, AIR 1996 SC 2969, 2976.
20. *Vellore Citizens' Welfare Forum v. Union of India*, AIR 1996 SC 2715, 2721.
21. A.P. *Pollution Control Board v. Prof. M.V. Nayadu*, AIR 1999 SC 812, 819.
22. *State of Himachal Pradesh v. Ganesh Wood Products*, AIR 1996 SC 149, 159, 163.
23. M.C. *Mehta v. Kamalnath*, 1997 (1) SCC 388.
24. C.M. Jariwala, "Complex Enviro-Techno Science Issues: Judicial Direction" in 42 JILI (2000) 29 at 36-37.
25. S.C. Shastri, *Environmental Law in India*, Eastern Book Company, Lucknow, 2005, p. 62.
26. *Subhash Kumar v. State of Bihar*, AIR 1991 SC 420: 1991 (1) SCC 598 in Kaarthikeyan, D.R., Environment and Human Rights, *International Journal of Environmental Consumerism*, Vol. 1, 2005, p. 86.

Bibliography

Basu, Durga Das, *Human Rights in Constitutional Law*, Prentice-Hall of India Pvt. Ltd., New Delhi, 1994.

Baxi, Upendra, *The Future of Human Rights*, Oxford University Press, New Delhi, 2009.

Birnie, P.W. and Boyle, A.E., *International Law and the Environment*, Oxford University Press, New Delhi, 2004.

Brownlie, I., *Basic Document in Human Rights*, Oxford University Press, Oxford, 1971.

Divan, S. and Rosencranz, A., *Environmental Law and Policy in India*, Oxford University Press, New Delhi, 2004.

Dube, M.P. and Neeta Bora, (eds.), *Perspectives on Human Rights*, Anamika Publishers and Distributors Pvt. Limited, New Delhi, 2000.

Griffin, James, *On Human Rights*, Oxford University Press, Oxford, 2008.

Jaswal, P.S., *Environmental Law*, Pioneer Publication, Allahabad Law Agency, New Delhi, 2004.

Kaarthikeyan, D.R., "Environment and Human Rights", *International Journal of Environmental Consumerism*, Vol. 1, 2005.

Nayak, R.K., "International Environment and Human Rights Law and Policy: A Perspective on Environmental Consumerism", *International Journal of Environmental Consumerism*, Vol. 1, 2005.

Nimushakavi, V., *Constitutional Policy and Environmental Jurisprudence in India*, Macmillan India Ltd., 2006.

Sanajaoba, N., *Human Rights in the New Millennium*, Manas Publications, New Delhi, 2004.

Sen, A.N., *Human Rights*, Sri Sai Law Publications, Faridabad, 2002.

Shastri, S.C., *Environmental Law in India*, Eastern Book Company, Lucknow, 2005.

Verma, J.S., *The New Universe of Human Rights*, Universal Law Publishing Co. Pvt. Ltd., New Delhi, 2004.

Vijapur, Abdul Rahim P., *The United Nations at Fifty: Studies in Human Rights*, South Asian Publishers, New Delhi, 1996.

Vijapur, A.P. and Kumar Suresh, (ed.), *Perspectives on Human Rights*, Manak Publications, New Delhi, 1999.

Index